Water
GARDENS

A Guide to Creating, Caring for, and Enjoying Aquatic Landscaping

Teri Dunn

FRIEDMAN/FAIRFAX
PUBLISHERS

A FRIEDMAN/FAIRFAX BOOK

© 1997 by Michael Friedman Publishing Group, Inc.

Library of Congress Cataloging-in-Publication Data available upon request.

ISBN 1-56799-509-8

Editor: Susan Lauzau
Art Designer: Andrea Karman
Photography Editor: Amy Talluto
Production Manager: Karen Matsu Greenberg

Color separations by Ad. Ver. srl.
Printed and bound in China

1 3 5 7 9 10 8 6 4 2

For bulk purchases and special sales, please contact:
Friedman/Fairfax Publishers
Attention: Sales Department
15 West 26th Street
New York, New York 10010
212/685-6610   FAX 212/685-1307

Visit our website:
http://www.metrobooks.com

Photography Credits:
©Cathy Wilkinson Barash: 97, 107 right
©Todd Davis: 62 both, 69, 110
Envision/© Henryk T. Kaiser: 100; ©Priscilla Connell: 8
©Derek Fell: 23, 34, 37 left, 74, 75 all, 77, 79, 89, 93 all
©John Glover: 13, 15 left, 16, 24, 25, 26, 31, 32, 44, 70, 81, 82, 87, 90, 107 left, 113, 116
©Adam Jones: 40
©Dency Kane: 41, 59, 65 left, 73

©Charles Mann: 2, 11, 30, 36, 37 right, 38, 39, 42, 43, 45, 50-51 all, 55, 56-57, 60, 63, 64
©Clive Nichols: 6, 10, 12, 14, 18, 28, 48, 58, 65 right, 66, 67 both, 80, 86, 88, 101, 102
©Jerry Pavia: 27, 35, 61 both, 68, 106 left, 108, 112, 114, 115
Photo/Nats: © Hal Horwitz: 72; © Don Johnston: 83; © Virginia Twinam-Smith: 104
©Tim Street-Porter (garden design by Nancy Goslee Power): 29
©Judy White: 15 right, 17, 54, 71, 106 right, 118

This book is dedicated with love and admiration to my friend and water-gardening mentor, W. C. (Bill) Frase.

I've used his good advice to be "thorough, constant, neat, and patient," not just when gardening but when writing this book—

and in my life in general.

Special thanks for all your help and encouragement over the years: John and Mary Mirgon, Joe Tomocik,

and Anita and Rolf Nelson.

And to Shawn and Wes, with love.

CONTENTS

Preface 8

Chapter 1   What Kind of Pool Is for You?   10

Chapter 2   Planning and Installation   34

Chapter 3   Stocking and Planting   58

Chapter 4   Maintenance   80

Chapter 5   Plants for the Water Garden   100

Appendices Equipment Options   120

   Fish Matters   121

   Water Quality   124

Mail-Order Suppliers   126

Water Gardening Networks and Resources   126

Further Reading   127

Plant Hardiness Zones   127

Index   128

PREFACE

"Turtle and fish and the pinpoint chirpings of individual frogs are all watery projections, concentrations—of that indescribable and liquid brew which is compounded in varying proportions of salt and sun and time. It has its appearances, but at its heart lies water...which shelters and brings into being nine tenths of everything alive."

—Loren Eiseley,
The Immense Journey, 1946

"Water in a landscape is as a mirror to a room. The feature doubles and enhances all its charms. Whoever may possess a lake, a pond, or a pool to catch the sunbeams, duplicate the trees and flowers on its bank, reflect the moon, and multiply the stars, surely will."

—Neltje Blanchan, *The American Flower Garden*, 1909

Water gardening has become an exciting new trend. Even very small properties now lay claim to pools. Tub gardens are on display at public gardens. Waterlilies, water iris, and taro plants are sprouting up in tanks at commercial garden centers. Landscape architects are enthusiastically touting "water features." Streams, ponds, and boggy areas of properties, once the cause of uncertainty and dismay, are now seen as opportunities rather than problem spots, places where water-loving plants can shine. Gardening magazines regularly feature enticing examples of water gardens. And maybe you've passed by someone's property in midsummer and admired, quite visible from a distance, the lush rainbow of color so well provided by a well-stocked water garden. The word is out: Water gardening needn't be a tricky, nor a prohibitively expensive, hobby.

In fact, water gardening is surprisingly easy, and it gives back a lot of pleasure for less effort than you might think, making it ideal for today's busy lifestyles. The new technology—in the form of affordable, durable, easy-to-install liners, easy-to-maintain pumps, and so on—is available to any gardener. The wish to be more ecologically sensitive is answered by water gardening, too. A water garden uses significantly less water than the same area covered by lawn (some estimate one-tenth as much); it requires little fertilizer; it may never require pesticides or herbicides; and it creates sanctuary for many creatures, both those you introduce to it and those that invite themselves. Caring for waterlilies and other aquatic plants is not very taxing simply because that most basic need—ample water—has already been met. And the beginner's greatest anxiety, the appearance of algae, is frequently resolved effortlessly, by doing nothing; in a short while, the combined elements find their natural balance, the spreading waterlily pads cover the water's surface, and the green invasion subsides on its own.

Yes, a water garden involves an initial investment in money and time. But if you plan wisely and appropriately for your garden, your needs, and your budget, you'll find few additional outlays necessary in the years to come. A quality liner (and good equipment, if you choose to invest in some) will last many years. Many water plants, and even fish, can be overwintered if you don't want to buy new ones every year. If you are daunted by the prospect of the installation of a water garden, you can certainly hire a qualified landscaper, although that will drive up the cost. Before you hire assistance, read on. There is no reason why you can't put in a garden pool on your own and have a very professional-looking job to show off. But with or without help, you'll be delighted with your gorgeous, low-maintenance garden.

A water garden comes to life with gusto late every spring, even the very first spring, and it provides constant and splendid color all summer long and into autumn. Not even your shrubs and perennials can do that. At its simplest, a waterlily pool is a concentration of beautiful color. There is something quite primal about water that draws us to it. When you have a water garden, you find yourself visiting it practically daily. The rest of the day's garden chores done (or not), you will invariably detour to crouch or kneel for a time at the pool's edge. You'll admire the perfect beauty of an open waterlily blossom. You'll watch bees working their way earnestly from blossom to blossom. You'll notice that one of your water cannas is about to unfurl several gorgeous, fiery red blooms. You'll see the wind's gentle ripples on the water's surface, and the comings and going of clouds overhead. You'll peer below the surface to glimpse the wanderings of the fish.

A water garden is a small habitat unto itself. It certainly may be said of water gardens, "If you build it, they will come!" It attracts a range of animals and insects with the promise of food and shelter, and in an age when natural habitats are shrinking in the face of urban and suburban development, many creatures are grateful for a refuge. And so your pool, although technically an artificial environment, will become a sanctuary. A healthy water garden will develop into a microcosm. The cycles of nature will be readily apparent: creatures reproducing, eating, and being eaten; plants coming into bloom, fading, and setting seed or sending out runners. In time, a natural balance will be struck, and you'll feel less like a little creator and more like a respectful witness.

Tending a water garden over a summer is an enjoyable ritual, and far from hard work. Simply trim off fading leaves and blossoms so they don't decay in the water, and don't worry about being perfectly meticulous; the pool will be able to handle the few you may miss. When the water level drops slightly due to evaporation on hot days, top it off with the hose. Fertilize waterlilies and other flowering plants in pots monthly. Clip a just-opening waterlily bud or two to bring indoors and float in a bowl of water; in a warm room, the blooms will open in a few hours. Feed the fish every now and then (they will help themselves to insects). That's about it.

Few hobbies, even in the gardening world, are more absorbing, satisfying, and perhaps healing than water gardening. This is much more than a fondness for beauty, which any gardener can rightly be charged with indulging in. No, it has more to do with water itself, with properties essential and somewhat magical. Pausing at the pool's edge, you will come to understand that you too, no less than the plants and animals that dwell within, need water. A water garden reminds us about nature's rhythms, the intimacy of the Earth, the vastness of the sky, our importance and our insignificance. Jarring noises and distractions drop away. In a busy and troubled world, something as simple as a backyard pool is a balm to the human spirit.

This book is intended to show you how to get started, and should answer questions you may have once you're up and running. You'll learn how to install and maintain a water garden you can be proud of and enjoy for years to come. As with anything else, the more you learn about water gardening, the more you may want to know. For further information, refer to page 126 for a list of specialty mail-order catalogs that offer plants, supplies, and fish (and often seasoned advice as well). Addresses of helpful organizations and the other resources are also provided. Happy water gardening!

Teri Dunn
Medford, Oregon

Chapter 1

WHAT KIND OF POOL

IS FOR YOU?

Decisions, choices, things to consider

*N*o doubt about it, putting in a water garden is a big decision. While it isn't irrevocable (taking one out is about as much work as eradicating an established perennial border), you don't want to find yourself in that position. In order to get it right the first time, you need to make informed choices.

Right out of the gate, you need to decide whether your pool will emphasize plants or fish, because this will dictate

what you install. Fish ponds are generally deeper, require extra maintenance and filtering equipment, and may limit your plant choices (see Fish Matters, page 121, for information on what is involved). If a lush display of waterlilies and other aquatic plants is your wish, then provide a good home for them by selecting a pool of appropriate size and depth.

Above: Even the smallest in-ground pool has the power to transform. If your garden has a lush, informal feel, a pool with an irregular shape—teardrop, kidney, or "amoeba," to name a few of the many styles possible—is best. Although it doesn't seem like much, just one or two waterlilies and a handful of pretty marginal plants can quickly fill a small pool. The result? A natural-looking display that will be your pride and joy.

〜〜〜

Opposite: Water has a way of immediately lending grandeur and a sense of calm to a formal garden setting. Here, the landscaper wisely constructed the pool to echo the shape and feel of the sitting area, for a harmonious picture that invites contemplative viewing. And like a mirror in a small room, the flat reflecting surface makes the whole garden seem somehow larger than it actually is. Note also how the plants on the perimeter help integrate the pool into the garden proper, both with their reflections and by softening the transition.

CONTAINER WATER GARDENS

Starting small before committing yourself to a big project is always wise. Before you dig a hole in the backyard, consider introducing yourself to water gardening by planting a tub garden. All you need for this is a watertight container and a sunny, level spot. However, unlike big pools, tub gardens aren't naturals for the center of a lawn. They end up looking dwarfed or out of place, and because it's impossible to mow right up to the edge, they acquire a somewhat scruffy look (unless you're awfully good with grass shears). Better to place your container water garden next to a wall, fence, or arbor, where it will capture attention and enjoy a little shelter from blazing noonday sun and high winds.

If you specifically want to grow a waterlily in a tub garden—and a number of hardy ones grow well and bloom profusely even in a restricted space—select a container 2 or 3 feet (60 to 90cm) wide and deep. Many other aquatic plants will do just fine in smaller containers and give you a taste of just how easy and satisfying water gardening can be. (In Chapter Five, Plants for the Water Garden, scan the lists for those described as suitable for containers.) Don't err on the side of too small a container, because water heats up when confined to a small space, and while most aquatics like warm water, they won't enjoy hot water. Also, if you add fish, overheated water is sure to cook them. No matter what size container you choose, remember that water is heavy—more

than 8 pounds (3.5kg) per gallon (4 L)—and even a small tub can become backbreaking to move. Fill it after you've settled it in its location. If the display is planned for a deck, patio, or balcony, be sure the supporting structure can take the weight.

For an intriguing look, consider sinking a container water garden into the ground in the garden proper. Just leave the lip an inch or two (2.5 to 5cm) above the surrounding soil so runoff from the garden is less likely to get in. Any visible part can be disguised and incorporated into the surrounding garden by mounding soil and rocks up around it, and perhaps even wedging in a few trailing plants such ivy or creeping thyme.

The most popular and perhaps the least expensive choice for container water gardens, and one that can accommodate a small waterlily, is the half whiskey barrel, available at any garden center or home-and-garden supply store for no more than $20. In their

"raw" state, whiskey barrels are not watertight, though, and are sure to leak. Also, the interior often retains residues that are toxic to plants and fish, and even soaking and zealous scrubbing will not remove all of it. A lining is a must. Basic hardware-store black plastic (generally 3 mil; you can double it for extra strength), carefully trimmed and fastened to the rim with a heavy-duty staple gun, works best, but isn't especially attractive. Some enthusiasts have developed clever alternatives, such as painting on a layer of rubberized or resin-based paint, or asphalt emulsion, or coating the interior with overlapping pieces of fiberglass cloth and using polyester resin as the "glue."

In addition to the small waterlily, a half-barrel garden can accommodate one or two of the taller water plants called marginals, one or two oxygenating plants, and some floaters. Pot everything in the smallest containers you can get away with, and keep excess

Opposite: Your imagination is the only limit when you recycle common objects for small water gardens. A discarded porcelain sink may be just the right size and depth to support some lovely water plants—here, bulrushes, jaunty Siberian irises, and miniature cattails make an attractive planting. Just make sure that any drainage holes in your improvised containers are well-plugged.

~~~

Below: A large round tub sunk into a circular raised bed of turf provides an easy answer to many water garden dilemmas. This container is large enough to accommodate a tiny bubbling fountain and several tall marginals, yet because of its relatively small size the garden is simple to maintain. The raised bed in which the tub is set prevents runoff from entering the container and the grassy edging furnishes a restful spot from which to admire the water garden.

Above: These days, there are many attractive containers available for use as small water gardens, including durable plastics that look for all the world like terra-cotta. Simple planting schemes are best; this one has been devoted mainly to pretty water snowflake, which has leaves that resemble tiny waterlily leaves and flowers like dainty white stars.

Opposite: Water-loving plants can be set directly in water and will thrive with a minimum of care. A number of favorite irises fall into this category. Here is the variegated form of *Iris pseudacorus*, always a popular choice for such displays. Thanks to its handsome, creamy yellow, striped leaves, this plant enhances a garden even when it is not in bloom.

Right: Containers can even become an integral part of a larger water garden design. Here, marginals are planted in square, wooden planters, which have been set in the shallows of a pool. The container is meant to be seen beneath the clear surface of the water, and lends a spare, Japanese look to the design. Realize that wood in water does not have an indefinite life span, so check the container periodically to be sure that it has not begun to deteriorate.

growth trimmed over the course of the summer. And be sure to elevate all the pots (on bricks or empty, upended pots, as explained on page 75) except the waterlily, which appreciates the deepest water you can provide. Finally, for good measure, add no more than two small fish. They will devour mosquitoes and their larvae, should any appear. The only significant pest mini water gardens seem to attract consistently is curious cats, who aren't likely to be capable of toppling such a heavy object, but can teeter on the rim while contemplating the fish.

While the half barrel is without a doubt the most widely seen container in use, there certainly are others worth considering. Some garden centers and mail-order water-garden supply houses offer stout plastic tubs that look like terra-cotta and old-fashioned kettles or caldrons, which can run up to $100. Even ceramic pots will do, provided you plug any drainage holes; in doing this, use a material that will stay securely in place when submerged in water, such as fiberglass, silicone, or even Bondo, the material used to make cosmetic repairs to auto bodies. Don't overlook nontraditional objects when searching for an imaginative water garden container. A ceramic umbrella stand—no drainage hole to worry about—planted with a single graceful specimen of cattail, umbrella palm, or taro, would make a unique and dramatic display. Children's wading pools offer possibilities, though you'll want to avoid the flimsy ones and examine your purchase thoroughly for cracks and holes before installing it. A sky blue bottom (or Mickey Mouse or Lion King motif) can be painted over with

Above: Fish or no fish? That is the question many beginning water gardeners ponder. While it's true that water plants and fish are often perfectly compatible, you must plan carefully so that everyone's needs are met. Large ornamental carp, called koi, are a great favorite because they are so beautiful and they make nice pets, but they require deeper water and regular feeding. You must also be prepared for the fact that they sometimes topple potted water plants or nudge them out of their containers.

a black rubber-based paint; such a paint adheres better if you sand the offending surface a bit first.

Metal tubs are acceptable, but they heat up especially fast and the water may get dangerously warm. If you have your heart set on a metal tub, choose one larger than 2 feet (61cm) wide and deep. Placing it in semishade or setting it into the ground helps moderate the water temperature, but be sure the plants you've chosen can still get the light they need. Or try growing a dwarf lotus, a plant that adores water at tropical temperatures.

Consider other recycled containers to make mini water gardens. All sorts of things have been used by creative gardeners, from old livestock water troughs to cast-off bathtubs, sinks, and laundry tubs. You can line or coat their interiors or plug them as necessary, as described above. If such "found" containers don't seem attractive, remember that you can sink them into the ground, construct a border around them (of rock or brick), or load them up with plants for a show so luxurious no one will notice or care what they're planted in.

So much for a first taste of water gardening. Later, when you've been bitten by the water gardening bug and have installed a big pool, your little starter gardens can make themselves useful as nursery or storage areas, or as places to experiment with raising young aquatic plants.

HOW BIG A POOL?

Starting small is not good advice when you set your sights on a garden pool. You won't want to go to the effort and expense of upgrading in a few years. (You may, however, want to install additional pools elsewhere on your property.) Many water gardeners look back and wish they'd installed a bigger pool from the start.

There are other advantages to putting in more pool than you think you want now. A pool often looks smaller once it's filled with water. If you landscape the sides, it seems to shrink even more. Plus, the larger and deeper the pool (within reason), the easier it is to care for. The water temperature is less likely to fluctuate, making for more contented plants and fish year-round. Smaller pools, as noted above with container water gardens, may overheat, encouraging the growth of dreaded algae and harming or killing fish.

DEPTH

All backyard pools should be at least 18 inches (46cm) deep in order for waterlilies and other aquatics to grow well, and for fish and other pond life to thrive. If you live in a cold climate and want to overwinter plants or fish, the pool should be 24 to 30 inches (61 to 76cm) deep. And if you want to include koi, they are best accommodated with a 36-inch-deep (91cm) pool.

WHY INSTALL A LINER?

Simply digging a hole in the ground and adding water, plants, and fish is a maintenance nightmare. Basically, it won't work. Unless your soil is especially heavy, the sides will cave in and muddy the water, and worst of all, the hole will drain out into the surrounding soil in short order. Granted, plastic and rubber remain environmentally incorrect, but a pool is one way to put these nonbiodegradable materials to a good, nurturing use. Invest in a high-quality liner so you won't have to replace it anytime soon.

PREFORMED POOLS

A preformed pool is a good choice for the absolute beginner. Yes, you are restricted to available sizes and shapes, but when you do a little shopping around, you will be amazed at the variety and should be able to find one you like. Preformed pools come in a range of prices, from affordable plastics to expensive fiberglass. Their sides are rigid, so you won't have to worry about creases and wrinkles, as you would if installing a sheet liner. Their tougher constitution also means that tears and punctures are unlikely to occur, and if exposed to sunlight, their edges will not crack or break down as quickly as lighter-weight plastics. Some can even stand above ground with minimal support. A salesperson will be able to advise you. (See page 29 for a discussion of above-ground versus in-ground pools.)

A preformed pool will require a hole that approximates its shape and size. Your main task once the hole is dug will be backfilling snugly around the pool in the hole. Note that these pools are best installed in softer soil, which allows for a little movement. Rigidity all around may lead to trouble later as your landscape subtly shifts over the years, which can cause heaving and even cracks in the pool. More nurseries than ever before, including mail-order ones, are beginning to offer these liners in kit form. This may include a small pump, filter, or both; a fountain mechanism; and even a selection of the appropriate number of plants, making getting started especially easy for novices.

FLEXIBLE, OR "FREE-FORM," LINERS

These give you the freedom to design the size and shape of your pool yourself. This option involves digging a hole and laying in a large sheet of heavy-duty, flexible plastic. No backfilling, no fussing over the fit. When you dig, you can be less precise because the liner naturally conforms to the hole. What you will have to contend with are some inevitable and unattractive creases and wrinkles. Installing this sort of liner requires more technical ingenuity. You'll need the right size sheet. You'll have to finish off the sides yourself, including anchoring them while filling the pool, trimming them afterward with a big pair of scissors, and installing an attractive edging that anchors and hides the raw edges.

Because these liners generally make for a less expensive garden pool, they are favored by gardeners who are confident do-it-yourselfers. But the project is not difficult, just big, and it is well within the abilities of anyone who has taken on other garden or household projects. Choose your plastic or rubber sheeting wisely, because this is a case where you get what you pay for. Don't buy the material found at hardware stores, as it may not be strong enough, fish-safe, or sufficiently resistant to ultraviolet (UV) light. Invest in a strong, flexible material that is intended for water-garden use. All liners have a life expectancy, and if your choice is not labeled with this important information, ask. Over long years of use, many liners will break down, thanks to exposure to harsh winters, chemicals, and UV light, as well as the occasional accidental tear or puncture. Naturally, the thicker the liner, the more durable and long-lasting it will be.

As for shape, you can imitate what you've seen in the more pricey preformed liners (kidney, teardrop, and so on), or make up something that suits your taste, your chosen spot, and the overall design of your garden. Just don't aim for something terribly elaborate, or you'll find the project quickly becomes difficult, from digging the complicated hole to getting the liner to conform to the hole to filling it with plants in such a way that it looks nice.

DO YOU NEED SHELVES ON THE SIDES?

Shallow shelves around the perimeter of a pool, a foot (30cm) or less down from the rim, are a useful part of the water garden. Generally 8 inches to a foot (20 to 30cm) wide, they provide a home in shallower water for pots of those plants that thrive in such a setting, the taller water-loving perennials known as "marginals." (Waterlilies belong in the deeper water.) Preformed pools generally come equipped with these shelves, and you can make them part of the layout of your free-form pool. Shelves are not mandatory, but they are a good idea if you want to include a number of marginals. It's easy to set the pots on them at just the right depth, and easy to tend to the plants throughout the season simply by kneeling beside the pool. If you need to go into the middle of the pool to add or attend to waterlilies or to check on a pump, filter, or fountain, you can remove some marginals and use the shelf as an access step to help you on your way in and out.

If you install a free-form pool, you will have the option of customizing. You can make your shelf broader if you wish (just make sure it's as level as possible so you don't have tottering plants). You can design the height of the shelf to accommodate marginals that require such special conditions, or put in a set of two shelves at different levels to accommodate a variety of plants. You don't have to ring the entire pool with shelves, either. A problem with a completely encircling shelf full of plants is that those on the near side may block the view of the rest of the pool. You may want a shelf only on the far side, or just at one end.

Despite their advantages, shelves are not without a down side. Water gardeners in warmer climates sometimes find them to be a trouble spot. The shallow water around shelves can overheat, harming the potted plants that sit on them. Hot, shallow water is also a recipe for rampant algae growth. If these are concerns for you, grow marginals in a straight- or sloping-sided pool without shelves, and elevate them on upended pots or bricks. Access to the pool may be more awkward without shelves, but you'll find ways to manage.

In all climates, the greatest problem with shelves is the access they can provide for hungry visitors. Many a water gardener has been dismayed and furious to observe a heron or egret step delicately down onto the shelf and proceed to dine on the pool's fish population. Raccoons and muskrats find the shelf a help as they clamber in and out on their destructive hunting expeditions, which may not only empty the pool of fish but topple plants. Fortunately, there are ways to discourage such marauders (see Animal Pests, page 95), and poolside shelves remain an excellent idea for most water gardeners.

LINER COLOR

The best and most widely available choice is black. It holds heat, it's reflective, and it recedes into the landscape. Also, it highlights your fish and flowers to best advantage. You may also come across green liners, which may strike you an attractive alternative. Like black liners, green liners have the advantage of not showing the film of algae that appears in an established pool. Baby blue liners are not attractive. They are too reminiscent of swimming pools and, to most eyes, look unnatural in a garden setting.

Liner Lingo

When you go liner shopping, whether for a preformed pool or plastic sheeting, you may become bewildered by the array of choices and technical terms. Here is a quick guide:

UV resistant: Resistant, but not immune, to decomposition on exposure to ultraviolet rays in sunlight. UV resistance is good, but it isn't a guarantee.

mil: This is not millimeters. It refers to a far smaller measurement, 1/1,000 of an inch, and has been traditionally used to describe the thickness of wire. Nowadays the thickness of plastic liners is described in mils; you may see figures ranging from an adequate 20 mils on up to a hefty 60 mils.

fish-safe: Refers to plastic that is not composed of or treated with any substance that may leach into the water and harm or kill your fish. Currently, all plastics identified for garden pool use are fish-safe.

PVC: Polyvinyl chloride, usually 20 to 32 mils thick. This strong plastic is resistant to punctures, tears, and decomposition due to sunlight exposure. PVC is usually the least expensive choice for a liner. Also available in two-ply form for extra strength.

EPDM: Ethylene propylene diene monomer, is a synthetic rubber plastic that is flexible, super-strong, and durable. It has excellent UV resistance. EPDM is considered a step up from PVC, and is becoming more popular because it really "melts" into a site and may come with a 30-year (or more) guarantee.

butyl rubber: The most flexible liner choice, which doesn't deteriorate from sunlight exposure. Generally available at 45 mils, It is considered the easiest to install and more durable than PVC. However, it can be difficult to find, and twice the price.

fiberglass: The most expensive material used in preformed garden pools, and also perhaps the longest-lasting. Suppliers will tell you that it lasts anywhere from fifty years to "forever."

Hypalon: A chlorosulfonated polyethylene, a tough plastic product that is most often used for inflatable boats. Not yet in wide use, it may offer even longer life than other liners.

Ulti-liner: A super-durable two-ply product an impressive 73 mils thick. Composed of 45-mil EPDM bonded to an outer layer of 28-mil geotextile material. It is considered to be state-of-the-art in liner materials.

CONCRETE POOLS

These are no longer as popular as they once were, thanks to the advent of the easier, cheaper, and more convenient plastic liners described previously. Concrete pools never were a practical choice for water gardens in cold climates, because freeze-thaw cycles lead to cracks and even heaving. Heavy reinforcing and a 45-degree slope to the walls can get a concrete pool through a cold winter; when ice forms, the sloping walls provide a chance for upward movement of pressure that would break vertical walls. If you don't want to chance it, you can always empty out all of the plants and fish each autumn *and* drain out the water—a lot of work!

However, if you live in an area where the soil doesn't freeze in the winter, this type of pool may be worthwhile. Properly installed with quality construction, concrete pools can last for decades. Consider your soil type. Concrete pools are easier to install and hold up better over the years when set into heavy or packed soil, which will provide some structural support. If your soil is very sandy or soft, the pool may experience minor or even major crumbling and buckling over time. As for soils high in clay, expansion and contraction can be a real problem.

Construction involves attending to several important details. First, the mix. The classic recipe, one that makes for a strong, long-lasting pool, is a 3:2:1 mixture of gravel, sand, and Portland cement, respectively. You don't have to mix it yourself—there are suppliers that will deliver it ready-mixed (check your telephone book's Yellow Pages). To ensure that the pool is watertight and long-lasting, the walls and bottom should be about 6 inches (15cm) thick. And you should pour it all in one day, without seams. Before you lay down the floor, install a large drain with a standpipe that can be unscrewed later for easy draining. Then lay the sides, working quickly but carefully. Prevent future cracking by installing reinforcing mesh and steel rods throughout, between two layers of poured concrete, like a sandwich. When you have finished, let your concrete pool cure for a day or so before adding any water. Mist the surface frequently during this period, or lay wet cloths over the concrete. If the whole process sounds daunting, you can certainly hire someone else to do it. If you are unable to find a local landscaper with garden pool experience, try a swimming pool contractor. The techniques and materials are similar.

Once your concrete pool has been poured, you need to prepare it for plants and fish. Because concrete is naturally alkaline, and lime leaching into the pool can harm the pool's residents, you'll want to clean it well first. This is not complicated. Just fill a mop bucket with water and a splash of vinegar, and scrub the pool with a heavy cleaning brush. Then hose off everything and continue adding water until the pool is full. Let sit a few days, then repeat one or two more times. Alternatively, don rubber gloves and goggles and give it a good rubdown with straight vinegar or diluted muriatic acid. Some people save themselves this effort by pouring the pool in autumn, filling it or letting natural rainfall fill it, and allowing leaching to occur naturally over the ensuing months. Come spring, they drain and refill the pool, double-check the pH, then plant and stock it.

It's wise to check the pH of the pool water periodically to make sure it's not too high. Early morning readings tend to be the most accurate. There are simple kits for this chore, available from water-garden suppliers as well as pool-supply houses. If the pH strays above 7, you'll want to allow for some additional leaching. Or, add some acid to counterbalance the lime (there are kits that you can use; just be sure to follow the instructions to the letter). Or buy a chemical that will convert the lime to an insoluble form; be sure to use a product designed for this purpose, and, again, follow the directions exactly. In time, though, rest assured that your concrete pond will age or "mature."

Once settled in, a concrete pool should be very little trouble. If it has thick sides, leaks should never be a problem. Some people hedge their bets after pouring, though, and coat the interior with a sealant paint or even just an additional pasty layer of Portland cement alone. If cracks should occur, you can seal them with these materials or with silicone or tar.

Above: This beautiful concrete pool adds a touch of elegance to a side yard. If soil and temperature conditions are right, a concrete pool can last for many years.

WATER FEATURES

Additions to the plain pool design are nice, and are best done at installation time. Of course, they all involve extra expense and effort. Here's an overview of the most popular ones, and a few words on what each one involves. For more details, see Equipment Options, page 120. Remember to keep scale in mind. One element should not overwhelm the others, and the decorated pool as a whole should blend with the rest of your garden's landscape.

FOUNTAINS These are generally the easiest to install, and are available in a great variety of sizes and styles. The important thing is to pick one that suits your pool's size and shape, as well as the overall feel of your garden. They add a wonderful dimension of rushing, bubbling, or tinkling sound—pleasant sound that may also mask distracting street noise in your neighborhood. Realize, though, that a fountain mechanism requires that you also buy a pump to run it. And, perhaps most important, be careful about where you place it. Waterlilies in particular dislike moving water, so you'll have to distance your fountain from the nearest waterlily by several feet, at least. If your pool is too small to accommodate both a fountain and waterlilies, well, you will have to decide which you want more.

Opposite: If you want water in a spot that is otherwise too shady to support a pool or even a plant-filled container water garden, try a simple fountain. Here a small bubbler has been tucked into a pretty pot (the pump that runs it is out of sight below the water). Not only is the display an attractive addition to an out-of-the-way nook, the soothing sound of it will be equally welcome.

Right: If your garden is not large, yet is densely planted, the presence of water might be just what the landscape needs. Here, by creating a "path" of water—sans plants—and embellishing it only with small, simple fountains, the designer has succeeded in adding a welcome respite for the eye as well as the ear. The scheme also assures that the large tiered fountain is a focal point—without the ribbon of water leading to it, the fountain might have been lost in the abundant vegetation.

WATERFALLS Again, there are many styles and ways to install these, and a recirculating pump will be necessary. The running and splashing water of a waterfall may be even more of an issue than a fountain would be for your waterlily population.

If the natural lay of the land in your garden doesn't really allow for a waterfall, you can pile up rocks or some of the soil you excavated from the hole, or a combination of both. Spillway lips, which go at the top of the falls and should be at least 6 inches (15cm) wide to assure a good, realistic-looking flow, can be purchased separately. If you are very ambitious and want a display that involves one pool spilling into another, take a look at what's available in the preformed liners, because you can find models where the spillway lip is part of the design. Preformed "cascade kits" are also available. In any case, it's always wise to underlay your waterfall with a piece of liner to catch leaking water and return it to the pond.

STATUARY You can choose anything from Greek goddesses to whimsical frogs. Select something that will not discolor, disintegrate over time, or leach lime into the water. Support it securely on a broad base so you won't have to climb into the pool to right it whenever it falls over, thanks to a toppling wind or a careless visiting raccoon. If you immerse it, its stand, or both, in the water, expect some water displacement.

STYLE ISSUES

ABOVE-GROUND POOLS First of all, think twice about installing an above-ground pool in a cold climate. The water will freeze, perhaps completely, possibly leading to structural damage such as buckling or cracking. You'll have to empty it of all plants and fish every autumn, and refill it every spring—an arduous, though admittedly not impossible, undertaking. Above-ground pools are good choices for gardeners in Zones 9 and 10 (Florida, southern California, and other areas with warm winters).

Having said that, above-ground pools can be dramatic and handsome additions to a landscape. They are easy to fill and work in, requiring less bending and stooping. You and your garden visitors can simply pull up a chair or sit on a bench to admire the whole display. They are untroubled by runoff, and even heavy rains will not cause the problems that they do with in-ground pools.

For an above-ground pool, you will have to purchase an especially strong liner. High-quality fiberglass liners are probably the best choice. Once filled with water, the sides of an above-ground pool have a lot of pressure exerted on them. So provide extra support, protect the liner from the sun's rays, and make it look nicer at the same time by constructing a wall around the perimeter, of bricks, rocks, or even timber. These above-ground pools tend to have a more formal look.

IN-GROUND POOLS A sunken pool's sides are supported by the ground, which also shields them from sunlight. In-ground pools lend themselves to a more informal look.

Opposite: The liner sides of above-ground pools need to be supported or shored up by stone, brick, wood, or another strong material. These reinforcements help the liner withstand the pressure of the water and prevent buckling. Happily, these materials also disguise the liner, making for an attractive water garden and giving you the opportunity to integrate the pool into its surroundings.

Below: In-ground pools are appropriate in any climate, but in areas with mild winters the water temperature is more likely to remain warm enough to support plant life year-round. This allows for a satisfactory show in all seasons. Also, if the water doesn't need to be drained at the end of the summer, the liner will be protected from the damaging rays of the sun and thus will last longer

But in-ground pools have their disadvantages, too. You'll have to dig a hole and find a place for the soil you remove. You may have to contend with runoff problems (water from the lawn entering the pool), though you can head this off at the pass by making sure the edges are a little bit higher than ground level. This has the added benefit of giving a little more weight and water pressure so that groundwater doesn't seep under the liner and allow it to lift up.

FORMAL WATER GARDENS These fit best into somewhat formal surroundings. Often they are the best choice for a smaller garden, where a strong hand on the overall design looks better. Think of the courtyard fountains of Spain, Mexico, or New Orleans, for example, or even just a small urban garden.

Formal water gardens tend to be based on a geometric shape: a square, rectangle, or perfect circle. Fountains and statuary are naturals for this sort of garden, which means you may have to sacrifice on the number or variety of plants you install. On the other hand, you'll enjoy the treats of graceful appearance, musical sound, and a focal point. You'll also be better able to enjoy reflections in the water's surface. You needn't eliminate plants altogether. You can enjoy a "splash of nature"—just make sure the plants you select are secondary to the artifice your formal pool displays.

For larger formal gardens, the Japanese look is popular. If that is your plan, study examples for ideas about shape, accessories, and surrounding landscaping (even if only in photographs in books). The artist Claude Monet's garden at Giverny, France, is often imitated, complete with green arching bridge; it has been the inspiration for successful gardens on a smaller scale. Monet favored waterlilies exclusively; such "monoculture" plantings seem to have a more formal air, even if the plants are growing lustily. Alternatively, create a monochromatic planting scheme, using all white flowers, or all lavenders. If you must or choose to site your water garden in a spot that doesn't receive a great deal of sunlight, you'll have to forgo waterlilies and perhaps other flowering aquatics, but you can make quite an elegant display of nothing but intriguing green foliage plants.

Opposite: Statuary is a natural addition to formal water gardens. Choose quality statuettes and fountains, avoiding those that contain limestone; they will leach damaging lime into the water and will disintegrate over time. And remember to support your angels or nymphs securely within the pool so you will not have to climb in periodically to right them.

Below: Rectangular and square pools always look more formal, and should be sited, edged, and planted accordingly. In particular, refrain from adding too many plants or combining them liberally—you'll only detract from the pool's elegant lines. Here, separate groupings of various water plants bring a splendid grace to the conventional design.

Opposite: Well-chosen accessories can greatly enhance the mood of your water garden. Here, the statue's contemplative gaze lends an air of discovery to his demeanor, as if he had wandered upon the scene and sat down to enjoy it. His placement behind some lushly growing plants (rather than out in the open) keeps the focus on the garden rather than on him. The statue's overall effect, then, is to invite the visitor to pause and gaze quietly.

INFORMAL WATER GARDENS More casual in shape, and more versatile for planting schemes of all kinds, informal pools are a wonderful addition to any garden. Landscaping tastes seem to run in cycles, and these days the more "natural" look is popular (even though the wise gardener knows that a "wild" effect requires effort). Pools in kidney, teardrop, lagoon, and "amoeba" shapes are just a few of the many variations you can buy or fashion yourself. They have a more natural feel to them and, once established, can give the impression they've always been there.

To give your informal pool that desirable "always been there" look, take a cue from nature. Natural ponds tend to have plants growing in the shallow water as well as plants growing on the banks. This transitional effect is easy to imitate. Place pots of marginals on the side shelves (or up on supports so they're still in the shallow water they require), and grow moisture-loving plants of compatible appearance adjacent to your pool, such as arching ferns or maybe a small Japanese maple with a graceful profile. (For more suggestions, see Chapter Five, Plants for the Water Garden).

Informal ponds can be accented successfully with some fountain designs or a waterfall. A rock waterfall will look better if the surrounding area is a rock garden or if there are at least some other rocks in the vicinity.

The sheer variety of plants appropriate for an informal pool immediately provides a lush, natural look. Feel free to experiment with combining various colors, leaf forms, and textures. When waterlilies and other aquatic plants that float or trail on the surface of the water are offset by what landscape designers call the "vertical accents" of marginal plants, your pool will be full of variety and interest. Just be careful not to overdo it, or your pool will become an unnatural-looking hodgepodge, "too busy," not restful to the eye whether seen from a distance or up close. Speaking of viewing your water garden, you will want to place a garden bench, several chairs, or even a stump nearby, where you and visitors can admire the display in comfort. This enhances the feel of a garden.

FOCAL POINTS Water gardens make natural focal points in a landscape. Water's mirrorlike qualities stand out at a distance and add dimension and depth to a landscape as nothing else can. We're attracted by the sounds and the movement a water garden provides, whether from a fountain or waterfall or even buzzing bees and flitting dragonflies. In short, a water garden is inevitably a mesmerizing, seductive feature.

There are two schools of focal-point thought. One is the "surprise" focal point, which in the case of garden pools can be achieved in a number of ways. You can locate the pool beyond something big or dramatic (a potting shed, a flowering tree, an arbor). When you include a waterfall or fountain, you can site the pool in such a way that people will hear it before they see it, and at that point, they will seek it as surely as a moth is drawn to a flame. A meandering path leading to the pool will add to the anticipation.

Or, make it easy and obvious to see and approach the pool—the "show-off" focal point. Site it out in the open. (There are practical reasons for this, too, which you will read about in the next chapter.) Don't place it in a landscaping scheme where it will have to fight for attention. Instead, place it at the intersection of two garden paths in the heart of a flower, herb, or vegetable garden, or in the center of a green lawn. Garden pools have a lot of charisma, and it makes sense to capitalize on that.

Chapter 2

PLANNING AND INSTALLATION

Step-by-step instructions

Once you've decided what sort of pool you'd like to install, it's time to figure out where on your property to site it. Wise placement not only makes for an attractive water garden, it means less maintenance down the line. Installation will proceed more smoothly if you choose an appropriate spot.

Compare ponds in nature with garden pools. In nature, ponds are often located in low-lying places. They are fed by the local water table, streams, and rain.

Your garden pool will be different. No matter how gracefully you blend it into the landscape, it will be artificial. So no matter how you construct it, it will not receive water from any source except your garden hose (with the exception, to a minor extent, of rainfall). Excess water will not be able to drain away naturally from your manufactured pool into the landscape, thanks to its impermeable sides and bottom.

Above: The thought and effort you put into installing your garden pool now will pay off abundantly later, once it's filled and planted. So choose your site with care, and invest in quality construction.

〜〜〜

Opposite: The best spot for a water garden is almost always right out in the open. You will be able to tend it more readily and admire it more easily, and the plants—especially the waterlilies—will get the full sun they need to thrive. Finishing off the edges with irregularly shaped stones will give the pool a pleasing natural look. Judicious poolside landscaping will help integrate the water garden into the rest of your design.

Too much water in a garden pool means an overflow, and sometimes a daunting mess to clean up. For this reason, locating your pool in the lowest spot on your property is a recipe for disaster. It ought to be on level ground, or if this is not possible, it must be installed so that the edges are an inch or two (2.5 to 5cm) above the soil surface. Otherwise, the pool will take on runoff water from the surrounding landscape, water containing soil that muddies the pool temporarily and settles into a layer of silt on the bottom that is a real headache to scrape out. Springtime floods are a fact of life, but the potential damage they can wreak can be avoided or mitigated in a garden setting if you consider the potential site carefully. Runoff water is also bad news because it may contain fertilizers from your lawn or plants that cause a burst of algae growth, or weed killers or pesticides that can damage and even kill plant and animal life in your pool.

Let the way plants live in natural ponds help direct and inspire the design of your water garden. Ponds in nature tend to be shallow near the edges and gradually grow deeper toward the center, with the deepest water of all out in the middle. This natural design transfers easily to the garden pool: your shallow edges can be accomplished with shelves along the sides, a perfect home for a wide range of marginals; waterlilies will thrive out in the deep water in the center of your pool.

PHASE 1:
PICK THE RIGHT SPOT

FULL SUN Waterlilies and other aquatic plants do best when they receive at least six to eight hours of direct sunlight a day, so choose a spot out in the open. A location suitable for a sun-loving flower bed or vegetable garden is ideal for waterlilies. When gauging the amount

Opposite: Here's an example of natural-looking edging. The rock slabs enclose the pool liner, and extend out over the water sufficiently to protect it. To keep the stones from moving, or wobbling when knelt upon, you must brace them into the surrounding ground, either by wedging them into a shallow trench or securing them into a mortar base.

≈≈

Below: The problem of runoff water from the rest of your property—especially after a heavy rain—is easily avoided. Just raise your pool several inches or more above the ground level. While you're at it, extend the edging out over the water slightly. This protects the liner from the damaging rays of the sun, plus provides a spot for fish to hide from any predators that may visit.

Above: The best garden pools owe their success to savvy placement. A level spot is critical (though if it's not perfectly flat, you can make certain adjustments during installation). Equally important is keeping the pool away from trees and shrubs, whose roots could invade its space and puncture or upend the liner. Also, shade from overhanging branches will not be welcome, nor will fallen leaves.

of sun an area receives, watch for cast shadows—the north or east side of your house, a neighbor's house, a substantial fence, or a garage or potting shed. (Also, beware too-close overhanging rain gutters and eaves that can dump dirty water and debris into the pool.)

As with most rules, there are a few exceptions. If you plan a smaller pool, it will heat up by early afternoon on a summer day, so a little shade cast on the spot at that time of day may be desirable. If the only site you have is less than perfect, you can still plan a handsome water garden with certain aquatic plants and give up on waterlilies (happily, a few lilies will bloom well despite some shade; refer to Chapter Five, Plants for the Water Garden).

AVOID TREES AND SHRUBS Shade isn't the only reason to stay away from overhanging trees and shrubs. Fallen leaves in a pool are a cleanup nuisance. And when they decay and sink, they can cause havoc with your pool's chemical balance. You'll want to steer clear not only of deciduous trees, but of pine, citrus, and crape myrtle trees, which drop foliage year-round. Petals from flowering trees and shrubs are less of a problem, partly because they're often pretty insubstantial, but mainly because they drop in spring, before the garden pool is thriving. Shed acorns, cones, and fruits cause less obvious but no less serious, problems; they sink to the pool's bottom and decompose out of sight.

Opposite: The purposely cracked pavement surrounding this pool has been planted with favorite rock garden plants in a scheme that looks charmingly unstudied. The low-growing rock garden plants don't pose any threat of falling leaves, and are a natural choice for poolsides covered by rocks or loosely laid paving stones.

Right: Choosing an open, sunny spot for your water garden will ensure success growing waterlilies, which need as much sun as most vegetables and herbs.

If you find it impossible to prevent garden debris from falling into your water garden, you'll have to skim often with a long-handled net, the kind sold for cleaning swimming pools. If clearing your pool of fallen leaves and other debris in your pool becomes a constant battle, or if leaves accumulate only in autumn, you can always lay a net down over the pool. Be sure to anchor the sides of the net well, so that the weight of the leaves or other material doesn't drag it down into the water.

Don't place your garden pool near certain plants. Some popular broad-leaved shrubs, among them mountain laurels, azaleas, and rhododendrons, have foliage that in sufficient quantities can be fish-toxic. Oak leaves, acorns, and pine needles all contain tannins that will leach into and discolor the water, and may also harm your fish. Avoiding trees and shrubs also ensures that you won't encounter large and difficult roots when you begin to dig your pool. Hacking or chopping them can permanently damage the

plants. And even if the tree or shrub survives unscathed, it could manage over time to put out new roots that might find their way back under your pool, possibly upending it—a scenario clearly to be avoided.

ON THE LEVEL You might not be able to site your garden pool in a perfectly level spot. On close inspection, few properties offer appropriate *and* level sites for water gardens. Minor adjustments can certainly be made as you dig your hole. Just remember that, unlike soil in a flower bed, water is not forgiving. It always responds to gravity and finds the level, even when your construction fails to.

Some water gardeners have successfully installed pools on slopes, shoring up one side. The steeper the grade, the more difficult such an installation is. To avert runoff problems in such a situation, you'll need to create diversion channels. However attractive the grade, though, never site your pool in the lowest spot on your property. (If you want to landscape a low spot, consider installing a bog garden.)

Above: Fallen leaves can become a real maintenance headache, especially if you installed a pool too close to overhanging plants that shed a lot. Often you can simply skim out garden debris with a net. But if the amount becomes excessive, the health of your pool and its inhabitants will be compromised. Gardeners who have to live with this problem sometimes install a catch-net over the pool, especially in the autumn.

Opposite: Good poolside neighbors are plants that don't lose much foliage or fruit. The problem of underground roots in the vicinity can be cleverly avoided by using potted accent plants. As for plants tucked right into the adjacent ground, choose shallow-rooted ones. They'll still require care, including watering, though a good mulch will help retain moisture and keep them in good health.

Opposite: Your water garden will be a focal point in your yard, so be sure to site it where you can visit it easily, and perhaps even admire it from indoors. While you're still in the planning stage, observe your chosen spot over the course of a day (to make sure it isn't too shady). And go inside and look out at it from various windows.

Below: Access to your water garden is an important consideration. You'll need to be able to get at the plants to groom and fertilize them, or move them around. These are more good reasons for placing the pool in an open area. This troughlike pool is an interesting variation on the more standard square and rectangular shapes.

ACCESS TO THE POOL Another good reason to have your pool out in the open is accessibility. Chances are, you'll want to be able to get at it from all sides, at least to maintain the plants. You don't want to have to be climbing in and wading over to the far side to accomplish these chores. In fact, it's wise to keep out of the pool as much as you can, for the sake of the liner's longevity.

AN EASY AND SAFE DIG Don't commit yourself to a spot without checking the soil first. Take a stab at it with a shovel and dig down about a foot (30cm). If it is hard as a rock, you've got a big job ahead of you, and you may want to change sites. Not only would be digging be arduous, but impervious soil is not very welcoming to a liner.

When the soil at the site of a garden pool drains poorly, expect constant problems. Water may get under the pool, leading to "bubbles" that are, at best, unsightly. They stress your liner more in some spots than others and make whatever is placed in the pool over them (pots, garden statuary, supports) wobble. At worst, these bubbles can push up your liner from below. Last but not least, make sure you're not planning to dig into utility, water, or electrical lines. If in doubt, call your local provider, who will be glad to come out to check on the location of supply lines at no charge.

BEST VIEWING Your water garden will be your pride and joy, so place it where you and visitors can admire it easily. Will you be able to see it from windows or sliding doors from inside the house? The drama of a water garden is greater if it is viewed from some distance, so you can take in *all* of it at a glance. Being able to see it from an indoors vantage point is also practical. You'll know when birds, welcome or otherwise, visit. You'll be able to catch unwanted guests such as raccoons or muskrats in the act (for coping with these, see Animal Pests, page 95). And a clear line of sight is also an important safety consideration: if a neighbor or visiting child should wander or fall into the pool, it's more likely that someone would be able to see and respond quickly. Garden

pools aren't very deep, as a rule, but it doesn't take deep water for a child to drown.

Outdoor viewing is another matter. All of the above concerns will be factors when you stand on the back porch, deck, or patio, but you should also be able to view your water garden from various spots around the property. For close-up viewing, a bench, some chairs, or even a picnic table nearby is nice. If your pool

includes a fountain or waterfall, the splashing will become more gregarious on windy days, perhaps even to the point of soaking onlookers if they are seated too near.

WIND AND AIR CIRCULATION As is the case with many garden plants, proper air circulation promotes good health in the water garden. For water plants, there are special con-

Opposite: In an imaginative and unusual design, the brick steps of this gazebo have been turned into a waterfall. The cascade of water becomes an integral part of the structure's design, and visitors are treated to the soothing sound of the water flowing smoothly down the measured steps. A side path allows access to the gazebo without wetting one's feet.

≈

Right: Provide comfortable poolside seating, and you and your guests will derive extra pleasure from the sight of your water garden. A few minutes will turn into an hour as you contemplate the reflected movement of clouds, the wanderings of fish below the surface, and, of course, the beauty of the plants.

cerns. Stagnant air around a pool allows the water to overheat. The exchange of oxygen between the water, the plants, and the air becomes stymied, and the plants may suffer. Under such conditions, fish are also likely to die. Sometimes a stiflingly humid August day creates this sort of stress, but as long as such weather doesn't last for more than a few days, the pool will rebound. Don't create or add to the problem by locating your water garden in a spot with poor air circulation to begin with, for example, very close to a wall, fence, or hedge.

Too *much* air movement or wind, on the other hand, isn't good for a water garden either. And not just because pots may be tipped over or garden debris will be dumped in the water. Forceful or constant wind can lower the pool's water temperature, sometimes abruptly. Many water-loving plants, and waterlilies in particular, prefer calm, warm water, and a wind-whipped water surface or cool water is not conducive to good growth. Plus, as mentioned above, wind can play havoc with such water features as fountains and waterfalls. If strong or steady winds are a fact of life on your property, you can take steps to minimize the effects on your water garden. Site the pool downwind of a windbreak of some sort (while staying out of range of the shade it casts). In the pool itself, some protection for the waterlilies can be provided by placing tall, sturdy marginals on the side or end of the pool that gets the first blast.

ACCESS TO A WATER SOURCE Try to position the pool within reach of your garden hose. This will make it easier to fill the pool initially and to top off the water level when necessary. If need be, of course, you can always buy an extra hose or two to extend your reach.

ACCESS TO ELECTRICITY If you plan to install a fountain or waterfall, you will need a pump, which must be plugged into an electrical source. Filters, available on their own and in combination with pumps, require electricity, too, as does any night lighting you might want to install in, around, or above the pool. But as everyone knows, water and electricity can be a deadly combination. Don't take chances. Consult a licensed electrician early in your planning process, listen to his or her advice, and get a quote. Unless you have experience with wiring projects, it is better to hire a licensed electrician to do the work for you. Remind him or her that all electrical wiring in a garden pool's vicinity must have a ground fault current interrupter (GFCI; see Equipment Options, page 120, for additional information).

MAKE SURE WHAT YOU HAVE IN MIND IS SAFE...AND LEGAL In most communities, you can install a garden pool without any permits, but it's always wise to give your local town or city planning department a call just in case. Among the codes you may encounter: a front-yard pool may be banned, or you may be required to fence it in to keep curious children and neighborhood pets at bay. There may be a regulation on the books about pool depth, though 18 to 24 inches (46 to 61cm) is generally permitted. You may be

required to site the pool 5 feet (1.5m) or more from the nearest building and electricity sources. Regulations are often directed at swimming pools rather than garden pools, so you may be able to slip through legal "cracks." Even so, you should still concern yourself with water safety. Fence your pool in, if that seems prudent, or landscape it in such a way that a child would have to climb over rocks, a berm, or lush plant growth just to reach the water's edge.

PHASE 2: DETERMINE YOUR POOL DIMENSIONS

DESIGN ON PAPER? Gardening books frequently advise designing an important addition on paper, and a water garden certainly falls into that category. But most of us are not mapmakers, and will be tempted to skip the graph-paper stage. One of the best suggestions I've ever heard is to photograph the proposed spot, then draw on the print using an artist's grease pencil. If you wish, take the photo to a print shop and get it blown up. Alternatively, you can draw a sketch from the photo. Either way, you will have an opportunity to picture your new pool more accurately.

EYEBALLING THE POOL A tried-and-true method for envisioning your garden pool in place is to outline its shape right on the ground. This is a simple matter if you know the pool's exact dimensions, as when you've picked out a preformed liner in, say, a kidney shape. If you're going to install a free-form pool of your own design, though, describing the outline of your new pool in the grass is a critical step, one that allows you to investigate a few possibilities and change your mind.

It's an easy process. Arrange a length of garden hose or rope on the spot, in the shape you want. Or, outline your pool with spray paint that can be rubbed off later. Use a measuring tape and take your time. Once you've "drawn" the outline to your satisfaction, stand back to get a better look. Walk around and examine it from all angles, and go look out at it from indoors. Check the proposed location over the course of the day to see if and when any shade falls on the site. If possible, leave the outline there overnight or for a couple of days. Installing a pool is a big decision that deserves some planning. It's not irreversible; you can refill a hole if you have second thoughts. But this simple step will give you a clearer idea of whether the pool you imagine will be as successful as it should be, and perhaps save you a great deal of extra work.

If you've already purchased a preformed liner, you could carry it out and set it on the proposed site. Don't drag it—get help. You don't want to scrape up its bottom unnecessarily, or your lawn either, for that matter. But, in truth, the hose or rope method will give you a sufficiently clear picture.

CALCULATING CAPACITY If you know how much water your pool will hold, traditionally measured in gallons or liters, you can plan how many plants and fish to put in it; as it is a finite environment, there are limits to what it will support. (This will be dealt with in more detail in the next chapter, Stocking and Planting.) The volume of water required to fill even a moderate-size pool may surprise you, but it will certainly fill with the hose the same day you complete the installation, and you won't have to spend that much water on it again anytime soon.

If you've purchased a preformed pool, the supplier will be able to tell you its capacity. In the case of a free-form or cement pool, you're going to have to do a little math. An exact figure may be tricky to come up with; curves (especially if there is more than one), sloping sides, and marginal shelves can throw off your number. For irregular dimensions, use the closest average dimension. Also, bear in mind that objects in the pool later, from potted plants to a pump, will cause some water displacement. Having said all that, here are the formulas. Although 1 cubic foot of water = 7.5 gallons of water, the number is adjusted for nonrectangular or nonsquare pools. For metric conversion, 1 cubic foot of water = 28.3 cubic centimeters.

rectangular or square pool:
length × width × depth = number of cubic feet; number of cubic feet × 7.5 gallons = capacity in gallons

round pool:
diameter × diameter × depth = number of cubic feet; number of cubic feet × 5.9 gallons = capacity in gallons

oval pool:
width × length × depth = number of cubic feet; number of cubic feet × 6.7 gallons = capacity in gallons

Generally speaking, 150 to 200 gallons (600 to 800L) makes for a small pool that may be prone to overheating in warm climates, but otherwise can be a good starter size. A 400- to 800-gallon (1.6 to 3.2kl) pool, however, is a better choice because it holds more and achieves balance more easily.

CALCULATING SURFACE AREA Sometimes it's helpful to know this number when deciding how many fish or scavengers to add. Here are the formulas:

rectangular or square pool:
length × width, then divide by 9 = square yards of surface area

round pool:
diameter divided by half (to get radius), then squared (that is, multiplied by itself) x 3.14, then divide by 9 = square yards of surface area

oval pool:
½ length × ½ length × 3.14, then divide by 9 = square yards of surface area

Above: A pool of any size requires a certain invest-ment of time, effort, and cash. Finding friends to help you with the heavy work will greatly reduce the amount of time it takes to dig the pool and lay the liner, and makes the task more enjoyable as well. If you are planning a large pool, like this one, having help is key.

PHASE 3: THE BIG DIG

Installing a garden pool is a project best done in spring or autumn, but not when the ground is sodden. You can certainly do it in summer, but that won't leave you much time to enjoy your pool that season.

It's wise to get help. As the old saying goes, "Many hands make light work." Digging a hole and disposing of dirt, not to mention maneuvering a liner, is hard work, even if the pool isn't all that large. Helpers are also valuable for providing extra eyes, handy every step of the way, but especially when you are working on refining the hole. Two people can finish this project in a day, or over the course of a weekend, depending on the pool's size.

The process of installing a preformed pool or a free-form one is pretty similar. You use the same tools, you dig and cushion a similar-size hole, and you finish off the project in pretty much the same fashion. Special steps that each type requires are described under the specific headings below.

MATERIALS AND TOOLS YOU'LL NEED:

SHARP, STURDY SHOVELS

WHEELBARROW

PRUNERS

CARPENTER'S LEVEL

STRAIGHT, UNWARPED WOODEN BOARDS (2×4s WORK WELL)

BUILDER'S SAND AND/OR OTHER CUSHIONING MATERIALS

TROWELS

GARDEN HOSE

INSTALLING A PREFORMED LINER

1. If you've purchased a fiberglass liner, you may wish to take the time to scrub it out with some soap and water before installing it, in case there is any residue of dust or toxic chemicals. With a plastic liner, dust is your only concern; just wipe it out with a damp cloth.

2. Set the pool on the chosen spot. The sides are slightly angled to prevent them from buckling or caving in, so your hole will need to reflect this shape.

3. Get out the hose or rope you used when planning, and make two marks in the grass: an outline of the pool's bottom, and of its top edge. The result should be a shape-within-a-shape design. (With more digging, but less precision, you may opt more simply

to dig a big hole that will accommodate the entire shape, and do more backfilling. Make the hole big enough so that backfilling does not become a tedious, close-in job.)

4. Excavate—see instructions on page 52.

5. Set the pool in the hole. Wiggle it into position, and use a wooden board and level to check that the sides are even. Double-check by removing the liner temporarily to see if it made a level impression. If not, add extra sand until it does. Add even more sand if you want the pool to be slightly elevated above the hole, which would prevent runoff entering the pool. If you've used some other cushioning material, it may be harder to be as precise. Take your time; you won't regret it. Return the pool to the hole and maneuver it into its final position. Use the board and level one last time to make sure the pool is even all along the rim.

INSTALLING A FREE-FORM LINER
In addition to the materials listed previously, you'll need:

4- TO 6-INCH (10 TO 15CM) NAILS

HAMMER

ROCKS OR BRICKS FOR ANCHORING THE SIDES

1. Buy or cut a sheet of liner of the right size for the hole you've planned. It should be at least 12 inches (30cm) larger (the overlap) than what you think you need, for insurance. It will look quite a bit bigger than the hole, but better safe than sorry. Calculate the width (widest point) and length (longest point). Then factor in the depth of the pool on all sides. The formula: (twice the depth + length + 2 overlaps) × (twice the depth + width + 2 overlaps) = sheet size

2. Excavate—see instructions on page 52.

3. Set your liner sheet out in the sun for a couple of hours before you begin, less if you live in the hot South. (*Don't* leave it on the lawn—it's heavy and hot, and the grass under it will suffer.) This

1. Outline the basic shape you want your pool to take, using a garden hose or length of rope. Then leave it there a few days and think about not only its location in your yard, but also its size and shape. Note that the site should receive at least six hours of sunlight a day to support most water garden plants, especially waterlilies.

2. Begin digging. Stay within your established boundaries, but angle the sides inward as you go so they slope gently. A 55- to 75-degree angle generally works best. Dig a few inches deeper than the pool's planned depth, to allow for a cushioning layer of a material such as sand.

3. Make sure that the top of the hole is level. Lay a straight, unwarped board such as a 2 x 4 across the excavation at various points and set a carpenter's level on it to check. If your pool is too big to lay a board across, place a stake or several stakes in the middle of the hole and measure from them out to the pool's rim.

4. Spread the liner out in the sun for a few hours, less if it's a very hot day. (Don't leave it too long or the grass underneath it will suffer.) This gives the plastic a chance to warm up, making it more supple—a more supple liner is easier to maneuver and mold into the waiting hole.

5. Drape the liner over the pool's cavity, taking care to distribute it evenly. The more help you can get with doing this—and eyeballing the results—the better. When you're finished, you should have an even amount of excess plastic on all sides. Do not trim this excess yet!

6. Slowly fill the liner with water. Creases in the bottom and sides are inevitable, though the pressure of the water will flatten them. You can keep creases to a minimum by patrolling the sides as the pool fills and gently tweaking and tugging where necessary.

7. Lay down an edging. This will serve several functions. It will anchor the sides and protect the liner from the damaging rays of the sun. And, just as importantly, it will make your pool look more attractive. Whatever edging you choose, take care not to puncture the plastic as you lay it down.

8. The reward for your efforts—a handsome finished pool. Let it sit at least twenty-four hours after filling so chlorine in the water can dissipate, or treat it with a neutralizing chemical (available from any pond supplier). Add plants first, and wait about a week for the environment to stabilize before adding fish.

gives it a chance to warm up and become more supple, making it easier to mold to the hole.

4. When the great moment arrives, carefully unfold and drape the liner in the hole. Distribute it evenly. The more people you can get to help you with this part of the project, the easier it will be. If you begin in the center, and unfold it one fold at a time, there will be minimal disturbance of your excavation. Once you're satisfied with how it lies in the hole, weight down the sides with rocks or bricks. Do not trim the excess from the edges yet.

EXCAVATION The process is the same regardless of which kind of pool you install. Spare your back by using a shovel of the appropriate length, enlisting help, and taking breaks.

1. Cut out and remove a shallow outline on the ground of the overall pool's shape. Now you can remove the hose, rope, or other marking you had laid down. Strip away all of the sod (to a depth of several inches) within the boundaries of your hole-to-be. Save it to use as patches as needed elsewhere on the property, or add it to the compost pile.

2. Start digging. Make the hole an inch or two (2.5 to 5cm) larger than the pool, excavating from the outer boundary down to the inner one, and try your best to match the degree of the angle of the pool side. In the case of a free-form liner, you'll have to angle the sides yourself. A good rule of thumb is to angle inward 55 to 70 degrees toward the pool bottom. Sandy soil requires no more than a 55-degree angle.

3. Remove the soil and haul it away in the wheelbarrow as you go. (If you just pile it to one side, you'll only have to haul away the pile later. Meanwhile, the grass under it will have been crushed—or smothered—if you leave the pile there too long.) Topsoil might be put to good use elsewhere in your garden. Subsoil can be used to make berms around the completed pool or piled up as a foundation for a waterfall, if desired. Discard all debris and rocks, and use a pruner to clip out any roots you encounter.

4. Dig a few inches (7cm or so) deeper than the actual pool depth. For preformed pools, the bottom of the hole must be level, so that the top of the pool and the rim all the way around will be level. When constructing a free-form pool's bottom, slope ever so slightly toward one end to make a spot that's about a foot (30cm) deeper than the rest. This will help you drain and clean the pool later.

Stamp on the soil at the bottom of the hole or tamp it down with the back of the shovel blade. Smooth it further with a piece of lumber. Scour the soil surface for any sharp objects now, before it's too late. Once the pool is filled, the pressure of the water on the liner will press it hard against any sharp object concealed in the bottom or sides of the hole, and that can result in punctures.

5. Make absolutely sure that the top of the hole is level. If the site is level to begin with, chances are this will not be a problem. To determine this, lay a straight board across the hole at various points and set a carpenter's level in the middle of the board. (If your pool is too big, place a stake or several stakes in the middle of your excavation and measure from them out to the rim.) If you don't get a level reading, it's better to add to or remove from the soil on the ground's surface than to change the depth of the hole. Just remove soil from the edges until you get it right.

If by some evil chance your pool turns out to be uneven, you'll find yourself emptying it out, removing it, and returning to this step to fix the problem. Of this onerous job, the English garden writer Nigel Colborn once remarked, "A dry liner is merely awkward to handle, a wet one is about as maneuverable as a beached pilot whale."

6. Prepare a base for the pool. The pool will sit more easily in the hole and respond better to fine-tuning if you set it on a base. A base will help cushion the liner from punctures caused by sharp objects, roots, or twigs that you might have missed, or from the intrusion of rocks that migrate upward in the soil over the course of a cold-climate winter.

An inch (2.5cm) or so of damp builder's sand (damp so it will pack down) is the usual choice for a base. Other materials work well, too. You can lay old carpet remnants, felt, tarpaper, or flattened cardboard boxes in the bottom and along the sides of the hole. A half-inch (1.5cm) or so of damp newspapers becomes a makeshift papier-mâché buffer. The most expensive choice—and the one that affords the most peace of mind—is invincible geotextile fabric, now offered by some water-garden suppliers.

PHASE 4:
NOW, ADD WATER...

Set the hose in the bottom of the pool and start filling it slowly with water. Once the first few inches (7cm or so) are in, aerate the water (add oxygen) as much as possible by holding the hose above the surface and allowing it to splash.

IF YOU HAVE INSTALLED A PREFORMED LINER Fill the gap between the liner edge and the hole's boundary with soil (sand on the sides tends to drift down over time) as the water fills the pool, using your hands and/or a trowel. Tamp it in with a trowel or board to make sure there are no air pockets or gaps. Work your way around a few times until the gap is filled evenly on all sides. This equalizes the pressure from the water and the soil and prevents bulges. If you've elevated the rim an inch (2.5cm) or so above the soil level, be sure to pack in soil to support that part, too.

IF YOU HAVE INSTALLED A FREE-FORM LINER Creases in the free-form pool's sides and bottom are inevitable. Water pressure will flatten them, and once you stock the pool, water and plants will hide or distract from them. You can keep creases to a minimum by adding water slowly, and patrolling the edges and adjusting the liner here and there as the pool fills. If need be, climb right in the pool so you can tug and tweak it (take care not to puncture it). Leave some ripples or creases in the bottom, though, to allow for flexibility in the event of earth movement—primarily the movement caused by winter's freezing and thawing cycles (or something more unlikely and drastic, such as

an earthquake). Because the water pulls the liner into place, you should not trim the excess liner until the pool is full. Leave the weighting rocks in place for now.

Once your free-form liner is full, pull the sides as taut as you can manage, and using 4- to 6-inch (10- to 15cm) nails, nail them down, right into the dirt, every foot (30cm) or so. This is temporary, just to secure the liner so you can finish off the edges neatly. When trimming, use big, sharp scissors and don't trim too much away. Allow yourself up to a foot (30cm) of leeway. You can always remove more later if you need to.

For information on installing items such as a filter, fountain, or pump, see Equipment Options, page 120.

ABOUT WATER If your water source is municipal, it no doubt contains chlorine or chloramine. This makes for safe drinking water, but it is not a safe environment for fish. In fact, it will probably kill them. Don't be tempted to stock your pool as soon as it is filled!

Chlorine will evaporate away on its own in twenty-four to forty-eight hours. If you aerated with the hose as you filled the pool, as suggested above, it should evaporate even more rapidly. Chloramine, a combination of chlorine and ammonia, is used by some water treatment facilities to make sure bacteria and other pathogens are killed, and it is much more resistant to dissipating. Call your local water district authority for information on your water supply. If chloramine is your lot, you must treat the pool water with a chemical (sodium thiosulphate) that detoxifies and neutralizes it; it's available in liquid concentrate form for a modest price from water-garden suppliers.

If you can't track down the information you need about your water supply, or if you want to find out for yourself what you're dealing with, use one of the test kits commercially available. Some tests check for the presence of chlorine and chloramine, and others also test the water's pH level (which should be more or less neutral, or about 6.8 to 7.4). If chloramine looks to be an ongoing concern, consider investing in a pond filter that includes a zeolite pad. Zeolite removes ammonia from chloramine, leaving the chlorine free to dissipate. Later, when you top off the pool to replace volume after natural evaporation, you shouldn't have to worry about the chlorine or chloramine you're adding at that time. It won't be a significant amount, and what traces do enter the pool will be diluted quickly. (If a problem does occur, i.e., your fish die unexpectedly, suspect the level of chemicals in the water supply; it can vary greatly between municipalities. In such cases, you'll have to be diligent about using a neutralizer every time.)

When you add water to your pool, remember that tap water contains little oxygen. Never submerge the hose in the water. Stand there holding the hose, or prop it up somehow, and allow water to spray into the pool so air gets mixed in.

One last concern about water: the temperature. The day you fill the pool for the first time, the water may be rather chilly. Not to worry. While you're letting the pool sit so the chlorine can dissipate, the water will warm up. As for topping off, always run the hose for a couple of minutes before adding to the pool, checking the temperature of the water first with your hand. If the hose has been sitting in the hot sun, the water can be downright hot, and you don't want to shock the pond residents.

PHASE 5:
DECORATIVELY FINISH
OFF THE EDGES

The edges (coping or border) of both preformed and free-form pools should be covered over or disguised after installation. Popular coping materials include everything from cement to rocks, flagstones, slate, tiles, wood decking, sod, and plants. The idea is to make your water garden look more attractive by giving it a finished look. But coping is practical as well. Plastic will break down—it will fade, then crack or develop holes—after prolonged exposure to sunlight's ultraviolet rays. Many of the new liners are rated "UV resistant," but that doesn't mean they're invulnerable.

Above: Rocks are always a popular choice for edging and accenting a water garden. Just be careful to choose ones that don't have sharp bottoms or edges that might puncture the plastic liner. Placed strategically around the edges of the pool, they give the water garden a pleasing, natural look.

Above: Edging a pool is both art and science. It is fun and satisfying to select attractive stones and place them along the sides. They will remain stable if you wedge them into a shallow trench, which you may also choose to line with mortar for extra insurance. Remember to leave spaces between the stones where you wish to run electrical wiring for a pump or lighting.

Coping protects the edges of the liner from sunlight. It also helps hold your liner in place, preventing it from slumping, which may not happen the day you install the pool, but can occur over time. Finally, it's a good idea to make the coping overhang the water by an inch or two (2.5 to 5cm). This further shields the liner while providing shelter for your fish, a place to dart to safety when the inevitable curious cat or hungry bird comes to gaze at the pool.

The first step is to prepare a simple base for your edging. Slice out a shallow, narrow trench several inches (10cm or so) beyond the pool rim, about an inch (2.5cm) deep and 6 to 12 inches (15 to 30cm) or more across. If you've installed a free-form liner, you may now trim the plastic edges for the final time, remove the anchoring nails, and once your chosen edging is in place, they will be effectively buried and anchored.

Edging may be simple or elaborate, depending on the look you want, and how much time and money you are willing to spend. There's no reason why you can't carefully lay down some attractive rocks or flat fieldstones, just as they are, all the way around the perimeter of the pool. Make sure none of them has sharp edges or points that could poke or puncture the plastic. A more secure edging is a good idea, however, if you expect to stand or kneel close to the pool's edge and don't want to worry about dislodging the coping. (You'll also notice that visitors always make a beeline right for the edge, and you don't want any accidents!) A collar of concrete will do the trick, though it will have to be deeper than the 1- or 2-inch (2.5 to 5cm) shallow trench recommended above. To be effective, the footer ought to be at least several inches (or up to a foot or 30cm) deep. Some people even go so far as to lay down a collar of galvanized metal (available at hardware stores) first, and put the mortar atop that. This is neater and ultimately more secure than slapping the mortar onto liner plastic or raw soil.

In any event, when laying stones or bricks, work with care, wedging them in place as snugly and evenly as possible. Remember to overhang the edge a little bit, as recommended. If you're using mortar, be sparing but safe. Too much will end up looking unnatural or sloppy, while too little will make it unstable. There is a small drawback to using mortar. It is high in lime, and if the lime gets into the pool water, it can harm your plants and fish. Neat work and careful cleanup will do much to prevent this from becoming a problem. Exposed mortar can be washed with a special solution (called "drylock etch") that effectively neutralizes the lime. If you are still concerned about contamination after using a lime neutralizer, you can always drain the pool and refill it.

If your free-form pool has a formal square or rectangular shape, consider bypassing the traditional coping materials and methods and edging it with a layer of up to four landscape timbers, such as 6×6s. (Be sure they're "untreated," because toxic preserving chemicals can leach into the pool and won't be welcome there.) Timber may well be faster and cheaper.

Measure out and buy the timbers in advance, and lay them on the ground before you even begin to dig the hole. You'll be able to envision the final result, and their presence will help guide your digging. Just remember that, like the pool itself, they must be level. If you find that they are not, dig shallowly below them as necessary. Fasten them in place with box nails and small wooden spacers, leaving small gaps if you wish to run concealed wires through for a pump or other accessory. Attach abutting timbers by drilling holes for 10-inch (25cm) galvanized spikes (available at lumberyards) or by nailing the timbers together. When you have finished, trim the liner flush, then drive long nails through the layers to hold everything in place.

Right: A successful pool installation owes a lot to careful construction—a little effort at the outset means no worries later. Here, the gardener has protected the pool from runoff water by raising it above ground level, and laid down secure edging that not only protects the liner's rim but can hold the weight of garden visitors. And by extending the liner edge over the water slightly, the koi can find shelter when they need it.

Chapter 3

STOCKING AND PLANTING

How to launch your water garden

The first lesson a beginning water gardener learns is that there are too many wonderful plants and too little pool. The temptation is great to put in all sorts of waterlilies and an assortment of interesting and complementary marginals and floating plants. Just as with a new perennial border or a vegetable garden at the outset of the season, it looks possible at first. But plants grow. And water plants really grow, some so eagerly that

in a matter of weeks they become invasive and must be thinned. They jockey for light and space, flower less or stop flowering altogether, and their leaves die back. Crowded waterlilies will rear their leaves up out of the water in a desperate bid for space ("pyramiding") that is neither good for them nor attractive. If you don't intervene, the pool becomes an unappealing, overgrown tangle. So keep it simple.

Above: There's much more to water garden plants than waterlilies. Here, a floating mat of delicate water clover makes a lovely picture at the water's surface. Each one is a mere three inches (7.5cm) across, and individual leaves are accented with white, yellow, or bronze.

Opposite: Though it's tempting to want to fill your water garden with nothing but beautiful waterlilies, the addition of marginal plants adds the excitement of vertical drama. Here, clumps of *Iris laevigata* enhance the lily pad display and help make the transition to the plants growing on land.

Take the first season to grow those plants that tempt you the most. Inevitably some will do better than others, and gradually, over the years, you'll refine your water garden's display. Or you may decide on a different theme from one year to the next—for example, emphasizing cool purple- and blue-flowered waterlilies and marginals one summer, and switching to warmer yellows and oranges the following year. Two things may keep you from this tack. One is expense. Buying new plants every year can add up, especially in the case of waterlilies. The other is that you may want to get more involved horticulturally. When you become interested in dividing, propagating, overwintering, and even hybridizing, you are bound to run out of space. So you'll spend what you can (or even slightly more than you can afford), as with any other hobby. You can give away or sell excess plants. You may

decide on additional container water gardens, or install another pool. You might even go into business, helping others install and stock their pools.

HOW MUCH WATER DO YOU WANT TO SEE?

Some people install pools because they want to enjoy seeing reflections in the water, images from the surrounding garden, and passing clouds. This pleasure isn't denied to plant lovers. Bear in mind, though, that a planted pool needs to have about two thirds of its surface covered with foliage, or else algae can become a problem. A way to gain surface area is to grow fewer waterlilies, with their spreading pads, in favor of more marginals, or keep after floating plants as they multiply, ruthlessly discarding excess ones.

Opposite: If you take your cues from ponds in the wild, you won't overplant your water garden, and it will look more natural. Waterlilies prefer the deeper water out in the middle of the pool, while marginals thrive in the shallower water near the edge.

———

Below: The floating leaves of water lettuce are velvety to the touch. When water droplets land on their surface, they bead up like quicksilver. This tropical plant thrives in garden pools and is a handsome addition to container water gardens. It is, however, an eager grower, so keep it confined—escaped plants have become a real problem in some areas.

Above: Horsetail is a hardy moisture-lover that grows beautifully in a garden pool, potted and placed in several inches of water. A primitive plant, it never flowers—its appeal lies in its stately green stems that are accented at regular intervals by black joints. Horsetail makes an attractive, dense screen behind other plants, and may need to be restrained by pruning if it begins to exceed its bounds.

Top Left: A thoughtful marriage of plant forms on land and in the pool can make for a memorable display. Here the straight, graceful stems of an aquatic rush are juxtaposed at water's edge with the exuberant, feathery profile of daisy fleabane and some cheerful yellow coreopsis blossoms.

≈≈≈

Bottom Left: The generous flower spires and variegated foliage of a moisture-loving hosta such as 'Frances Williams' lend enchantment at the waterside, where their cooling colors are a welcome sight.

≈≈≈

Opposite: Sometimes less is best. If your pool is small, don't crowd or complicate it with loads of plants. An elegant display can be made with just one or two healthy, hearty waterlilies.

WHY YOU SHOULD AVOID PLANTING IN THE BOTTOM OF THE POOL

Although growing directly in soil at a pond's bottom is nature's way, it doesn't work well in the home water garden. A substantial layer of soil, muck, or both at the bottom of a pool leads to dirty water, water that is impossible to keep clear; the problem is even worse if you have fish, because they love to stir up the bottom.

In such a setting, the plants themselves can become a maintenance nightmare. You may find it difficult to provide them with optimum depths. Those that get established will do so with a vengeance, spreading wherever they find a foothold and tangling with their fellows until pruning back their invasive growth becomes horribly difficult. Finally, from the aesthetic point of view, it'll be hard to control your display and position the plants artfully in relation to one another.

THE CONCEPT OF BALANCE

All garden pools can and should achieve the desirable state known as "balance," the stable point where plants and creatures support one another. This happens perhaps more easily and with more complexity in the wild, but is attainable in the finite environment

of a home water garden, too. You must exert some control at the outset, then stand back and let the pool do the rest, intervening only if something goes awry. A healthy pool—one "in balance"—has a sustainable amount of plants, fish and perhaps other creatures, and a *slight* tinge of amber or green algae. Oxygen produced by the plants is consumed by animal life, who in turn provide carbon dioxide for the plants. This is the cycle that occurs on a vast scale in the natural world around us, and it is a cycle that must establish and sustain itself in the little world of your water garden.

How long does it take for balance to occur? This depends on many factors, from the time of year to the intervals at which plants and fish are added—but you can reasonably expect a garden pool to reach this desirable state of equilibrium after a month or so. How long can you expect your pool to stay in balance? Assuming you care for the pool and its residents properly, it will remain in balance indefinitely. A newly installed pool will always experience a flush of algae at first, until the plants begin to grow and it naturally subsides. Whatever you do, *do not* succumb to impatience or panic and empty the pool and start over. The repeated introduction of fresh water only sets the process back to square one. (For more information on coping with algae, see Water Quality, page 124.)

Opposite: To look its best and to avoid being over-come by algae, your garden pool should mature to having about two-thirds of its surface covered by plant growth. Waterlily pads can take care of much of this requirement, but other aquatic plants can and should contribute—they'll make the display exciting by adding contrasting textures, colors, and forms.

⁓

Below: Just one or two waterlily plants can end up consuming quite a bit of pool space, so always allow for mature size. Here, the tropical waterlily 'Shirley Bryne', sporting deep raspberry-sherbet pink blooms, casts its leaves outward to a spread of up to six feet (1.8m).

Above: There are many irises suitable for use in a home water garden and, as in the garden proper, you can count on them to provide not only beautiful flowers in season, but attractive foliage the rest of the time. Pictured is the flag iris, *Iris pseudacorus.*

Opposite: Tropical plants like the large-leaved, bright-flowered aquatic cannas are easy to grow and bring real splendor wherever they are placed. The orange one here is called 'Wyoming' and the red, 'King Humbert', but there are many choices in the red-orange-yellow range. Nor are these plants for mild-climate gardeners only; those who live in colder areas can treat cannas as annuals or over-winter them in a warm greenhouse.

Below: Also suitable for the water garden are varieties of *Iris laevigata*. (The red flower blooming in the foreground is the moisture-loving monkey flower, *Mimulus* 'Wisley Red'.) To keep them flowering well, you should divide your irises every season.

Above: Perhaps the most stunning of all primroses, and also arguably the easiest to grow, are moisture-loving candelabra primroses. They come in a broad range of splendid colors, from creamy white to pale pink to scarlet to various shades of purple, and feature contrasting eyes. They self-sow with abandon, so you are sure to enjoy them more with each passing year. No pondside should be without them.

ACHIEVING TWO-THIRDS COVERAGE

It's easy to hold algae at bay, a step toward keeping your pool in balance: see to it that the majority of the water surface is shielded by foliage. The often-quoted figure is two-thirds coverage, but more or less may do the trick, depending on your pool's locale, depth, and the season. The goal is to reduce the amount of sunlight that reaches the pool (algae adores loads of sunlight, and can't thrive in shade or darkness), while providing an accommodating habitat for your pool creatures. The best plants for quick coverage are waterlilies, as you may have guessed by now. Water hyacinths (*Eichhornia crassipes*) and water hawthorn (*Aponogeton distachyus*), where allowed (some Southern states have banned them), are practical, and are also fast, effective spreaders. Your main concern when planting these species will not be having too few, but too many.

Opposite: Making sure that much of your water garden is planted will help cut down on the profusion of algae that can grow if the pool's balance slips out of control. Here, waterlilies and water clover provide coverage that cuts down on the amount of sunlight the algae receives; along with papyrus, arrowhead, and water canna, they offer hiding places for fish who eat algae.

~~~

Below: Tropical waterlilies are easy to recognize because they tend to hold their large, magnificent flowers on strong stalks several inches to a foot (30cm) above the water's surface. Although they positively thrive in areas with especially hot summers, gardeners in the North can still enjoy them. Just get them growing indoors early, move them out to the pool when the water has warmed up sufficiently, and fertilize them generously.

POOL RESIDENTS

Before stocking, make sure you know the surface area and capacity of your pool (see page 47) so you won't overstock. You can always add plants or creatures, refining the mix as you get to know your pool's needs and personality. The stocking principles given below are rules of thumb; approximate them as best you can. For detailed descriptions of specific water plants, see Chapter Five, Plants for the Water Garden—the following is an overview only.

WATERLILIES These beauties are practically synonymous with water gardens and, provided the spot you've chosen receives five to six or more hours of sunlight a day, you can enjoy them in nearly every color of the rainbow. They are easy and rewarding to grow, blooming gloriously all summer long once established. Begin your shopping by learning a little bit about each one's needs and habits.

There are two kinds of waterlilies, hardy and tropical. Not surprisingly, gardeners in colder climates have more success with hardies, and gardeners in areas with long, hot summers report spectacular results with tropicals. Even so, both can be grown in most parts of North America. There are differences between the two kinds, including flower size and color, but of primary practical concern to you at the outset should be plant size. Some waterlilies are naturally small, spreading out their pads to cover an area only 4 to 6 feet (1.2 to 1.8m) wide, while others, given the chance, will become enormous, spreading up to 20 feet (6m). Stock your pool according to mature size estimates, no matter how small the waterlilies may seem on arrival. If you must have one that you know will grow too big for your pool, try underpotting it. (See Pots and Tubs, page 72.)

Waterlilies perform several important functions in the world of your water garden. The pads provide shade that inhibits algae growth and shelters fish. Their presence helps keep the water temperature cooler and stable, while preventing excessive evaporation. Finally, waterlilies contribute to the pool's health by producing oxygen via photosynthesis. Few water gardens can afford to be without these splendid plants.

MARGINALS Due to their vertical growth habit, most marginals do not contribute much to surface coverage. Still, they have many other qualities that are desirable in a water garden. In addition to their obvious virtue of contributing vertical interest, they create attractive reflections in the water and they look handsome alongside one another and among waterlilies. They also help shade the pool at different times during the day, offer frogs and fish a place to hide, and are a popular stage for visiting dragonflies.

Many marginal plants flower, but—as with flowering perennials out in your garden proper—the blossoms will pass, leaving only the foliage on display. For this reason, select marginals with foliage you will enjoy all season. Some are grown more for their foliage than their flowers. There are dozens from which to choose, and they vary widely in size and shape. How many you put in your water garden depends chiefly on whether you have and utilize all of a side shelf, and whether their foliage and flowers will crowd out each other or complicate your display.

OXYGENATING PLANTS These vital underwater plants are the unsung heroes of the water garden. Don't overlook them! They help keep the pool water clear by filtering out nutrients that algae would otherwise feed on. Their presence is a boon to your fish population because they contribute oxygen to the pool environment, and their trailing foliage and roots provide a place for fish to hide from predators as well as an ideal spot to spawn.

Most oxygenators are grassy-looking plants that aren't especially attractive, but they aren't readily visible, either. An exception is the popular parrot's feather (*Myriophyllum aquaticum*), which has whorls of feathery leaves that sometimes breach the surface of the water and sway with any little current or disturbance (or, in the case of a tub garden, mount the brim and spill over). If you like the look, leave the plant be. A tried-and-true formula is one or

Opposite: Moisture-loving ornamental grasses (such as *Hakonechloa macra* 'Aureola', shown here, whose green and gold leaves are colored like bamboo) and hostas are both nice choices for pondside landscaping, because they look good all season and don't add the distraction of showy, colorful flowers to the scene. With this type of subtle plant scheme, the plants in the pool are free to command most of the attention.

≈≈≈

Below: A small waterlily can do just fine in a container garden. Pot it in the smallest possible container—such as a four-quart (3.8L) nursery pot—and periodically prune off the outer leaves as they exceed their bounds. Don't yank on the leaves when you remove them; instead, reach down into the water and pinch or cut them off cleanly at the plant's crown.

two bunches (several plants each) of oxygenators for every two square feet (30 sq cm) of surface area, but experiment to see what works for your pool.

FISH Darting fish are not only an attractive sight in a water garden, they're practical as well. Like the scavengers they are, they consume algae and organic debris. But perhaps more important, they eat mosquito larvae—and no one wants their backyard pool to become a breeding ground.

For common goldfish, the formula is one fish per 5 gallons (20L) of water. Koi, because they are so much larger, should be added more sparingly, one per 10 to 20 gallons (40 to 80L) of water. For more information, see Fish Matters, page 121. You must remember to wait at least a week before adding fish to your new water garden; this will allow the chlorine to completely evaporate and the pool temperature to stabilize. (See Chapter Two, Planning and Installation, for information on coping with chloramine-treated water.)

SCAVENGERS These, too, are unsung heroes, little creatures that are rarely seen but that perform valuable functions in the life of your water garden. Not only do they eat algae, but they consume decaying plant tissue and other pool debris. The most common choice is freshwater snails, available from water garden suppliers and pet stores that supply aquarium hobbyists. You may also wish to try freshwater clams or freshwater mussels, where available. If frogs appear in your water garden long enough to lay eggs, you'll welcome the help of tadpoles in moderate numbers. These little creatures will eat lots of insects. The formula is one or two scavengers per square foot (30 sq cm) of surface area. Wait a week or longer before adding these to your new water garden, so the chlorine has evaporated completely and the pool temperature has stabilized (again, if chloramine, not merely chlorine, is present, treat the water as described in the previous chapter).

POTS AND TUBS All sorts of containers will suit water garden plants, but for optimum plant growth and health, here are some guidelines. In nature, waterlilies grow in soil at the bottom of ponds. Garden hybrids will do fine in containers; nevertheless, they appreciate ample space, so the larger the container, the better. Because their root systems expand more horizontally than down, wide yet shallow pots are best. Plastic or terra-cotta azalea pots, wooden crates (of untreated lumber, and never redwood or cypress, which are toxic underwater), and even small plastic laundry baskets all are appropriate. When practical, clay pots are preferable to plastic, simply because they're heavier and offer more stability—so plants are less likely to blow or fall over.

In any event, be sure the container you select has a drainage hole, even though plant and pot will be immersed in water; this prevents gases from building up inside the pot. The capacity should be between 16 and 32 dry quarts (18 to 36L); the size of the pots depends to some extent on the size of your pool. A one-gallon (4L) pot is adequate for a small waterlily if your garden pool is made of a half barrel. Don't underpot if it can be avoided. (If you're deliberately underpotting a large lily as an experiment, be conservative.)

Some water gardeners use a single, very large container to plant two waterlilies close together, which is a good idea if you want to juxtapose two of complementary colors, or a day- and a night-bloomer. Because marginal water plants are taller and can become top-heavy with bountiful foliage and flowers, they are best potted in taller, deeper pots, that is, traditional nursery pots. The size will depend naturally on the size of the plant. Many can be started in 1-gallon (4L) pots. Nursery pots are also fine for floaters that need to be potted, such as floating heart (*Nymphoides*) and water clover (*Marsilea mutica*), as well as oxygenating plants.

Signs that you've underpotted a water plant are stunted growth and fewer or smaller flowers. Sometimes you can get away with too small a pot if you pamper the plant with fertilizer while keeping it pruned. But if a plant looks really unhappy, if its pot top-

Above: A mixture of horizontal waterlilies and vertical marginal plants makes for an interesting show. Paired here are the hardy pink lily 'Fabiola' and the always-graceful umbrella palm (*Cyperus alternifolius*). Because both plants are potted, you can tinker with the display as they mature, shifting it until you feel both are looking their best.

ples under the weight of excessive growth, or if you discover roots questing out from the bottom, take action. Divide and return only a healthy portion of the plant to the original pot. Better yet, give the plant a new lease on life by moving it to a bigger pot.

USE THE PROPER SOIL

Unlike other container-grown garden plants, water garden plants should *never* be planted in peat-based potting mix. It lacks the heavy dose of organic matter they love, and it is too lightweight to hold its own underwater, leaching into the water and contributing

Above : A healthy waterlily that is planted in a pot of the proper size and fertilized regularly should bloom quite happily. This day-flowering, butter yellow tropical—called 'St. Louis Gold'—is compact enough for smaller gardens, and sports leaves tinged with bronze.

to floating scum. Instead, use a medium closer to what nature provides in pond muck—rich, heavy topsoil or garden loam. There may be no need to buy it; you can harvest it right from a corner of your flower or vegetable garden.

HOW TO PLANT A WATERLILY

Tropical waterlilies grow from small tubers, while the hardies grow from thick rhizomes. Plant both in wide, shallow pots of heavy soil. Aside from the placement of the rootstock, the planting process is identical.

Note that hardy waterlilies can be placed in water as cool as 50°F (10°C) without trauma; tropicals, as you might expect, really prefer warmer water temperatures. If you put a tropical waterlily in water that is too cool, you may shock it, delaying or preventing growth and blooming. Wait until the water in your pool has warmed to at least 70°F (21°C).

1. PREPARE THE ROOTSTOCK. Waterlilies are sold bareroot, usually with a few leaves intact. It is important that the root never dry out, so place it in a bowl of lukewarm water as soon as you get it home. Keep it moist until you are are ready to plant. Carefully inspect the rhizome or tuber for viable roots, which are white and crisp. Use a small, sharp knife to trim off any brown, black, or limp roots (if there are a lot of these, you may have a dud). Sometimes there are tiny lime green or bronze leaves emerging from the plant's growing point, or crown. Leave them on.

2. PREPARE THE CONTAINER. Fill the container one-third full with the soil. Insert a waterlily fertilizing tablet (available from mail-order nurseries that sell waterlilies and supplies) or a handful of low-analysis granular fertilizer, such as 5-10-5 or 6-10-4. Some water gardeners crush the fertilizer tablet or mix in the fertilizer to spread it evenly through the soil, though this is not essential. Then, to eliminate any air pockets, fill the container to the top with soil and drench it until water runs out the drainage hole at the bottom. This may take a while.

3. POT THE PLANT. To pot the rhizome or tuber, remove a third of the saturated soil and set it aside. You may want to wear rubber gloves, as this is a muddy operation.

If you are planting a hardy waterlily: set the rhizome roots down in the pot at a 45-degree angle. Angle the rhizome so the plant has room to elongate across the pot and the crown points up. It's okay to place the opposite end flush against the pot if necessary.

1. Fill the pot with damp, rich soil. Always use heavy garden soil, preferably right from the flower bed or vegetable garden. Bagged soilless mixes are too light-weight for use in a pool and will only foul the water.

2. Add fertilizer. Tablets specially formulated to nurture waterlily growth are available from water-garden suppliers. Poke them down into the soil with your fingers, or crush them and mix throughout—either way, you'll get your plant off to a good start.

3. Top the pot with a layer of pebbles. These will help hold the soil and root in place and prevent them from drifting out of the pot and into the water. Any small rocks will do the job (though you should avoid using limestone pebbles, which leach unwelcome lime into the pool).

4. Gradually submerge the potted plant in the pool. Keep the job neat by tipping the pot in at an angle so the bubbles escape slowly. Waterlilies like to be about a foot (30cm) underwater, so if your pool is deeper than this, lower the pot onto some kind of support, such as a brick, flat-topped rock, or even another pot, upended.

If you are planting a tropical waterlily, look for a white line on the tuber. This indicates where the soil level should be once you fill the pot. Set the tuber lengthwise in the center of the pot, roots down.

Once the rhizome or tuber is properly placed, gently top off the pot with the reserved soil, filling it to within an inch or two (2.5 to 5cm) of the rim, all the while being sure to leave the growing point free of soil. To avoid air pockets, firm the soil with your thumbs as you work. Water the pot once more, taking care not to wash soil away from the root. Then top off the pot with small stones or pea gravel (again, making sure to leave the growing point exposed) to prevent soil from washing away once it is in the tub or pool.

4. SLOWLY SET THE POT IN THE POOL.
To get the plant off to a good start, place it in 6 to 8 inches (15 to 20cm) of water at first and move to deeper water over the course of a week or so. This allows it to start growing in warmer water. Ultimately, most waterlilies prefer to be a foot (30cm) or so beneath the water's surface. If your pool is deeper than that, place some bricks, a concrete block, or an empty, overturned pot on the bottom to elevate the plant to the correct height.

Lower the pot into the pool gradually and at an angle to allow any air bubbles to escape, then set the pot on its base. If the plant has a few leaves, gently position them so they float on the surface of the water. Within a few weeks, your waterlily will have adjusted to its new home. New leaves will soon begin to appear, and shortly thereafter the first blossoms should make their debut.

HOW TO PLANT A MARGINAL

Use heavy garden soil, as described above, and a deeper nursery pot. Follow the same steps as for planting a waterlily, including the heavy initial dose of fertilizer, and remember not to cover the crown with soil. When you slowly lower the potted plant into the pool, place it just an inch or two (2.5 to 5cm) under the water's surface. Shelves along the pool's side offer a suitable setting, or you can provide extra elevation by placing the pot on bricks, a concrete block, or an empty, overturned pot.

Tropical marginals should not be placed in the pool until the water has warmed up to at least 70°F (21°C). Both tropical and hardy marginal plants, especially if routinely fertilized, will prosper and bloom their first season and in subsequent seasons in your water garden.

HOW TO PLANT AN OXYGENATOR

Oxygenators are often sold in bunches of several plants each. Separate them into groups of two or three plants, discarding any that don't look healthy. Using a sharp knife, make a fresh cut at the base of each stalk (this is best done underwater), just as if you were preparing a bouquet of fresh-cut flowers.

Then, simply stick them into a nursery pot of heavy soil or sand. You can tuck them in one of the big pots with another plant, but keep an eye on them so they don't begin to crowd out their host. Top off the pot with small stones or pea gravel to anchor the stalks in place. Otherwise, these lightweight plants may slip away and float loose in the pool. If this happens, you can retrieve and replant the pieces.

Don't worry if there are no roots present at first. Oxygenating plants tend to be extremely vigorous growers. They'll take hold quickly. In due course, you'll probably find yourself trimming back excess growth.

HOW TO PLANT A FLOATING PLANT

Those that need to be potted will prosper if planted like marginals in a nursery pot. They may need to be elevated to within a couple of inches (5cm or so) of the water's surface. As for free-floating aquatics, planting couldn't be simpler. If necessary, trim off dead or damaged parts and rehydrate the plant in a bucket of lukewarm water for a few hours. Then, just toss the plant into the pool.

HOW TO PLANT A LOTUS

Before you commit yourself to growing the spectacular lotus, read more about it in Chapter Five, Plants for the Water Garden. It has special requirements you may not be able or willing to provide. Don't expect it to bloom for you its first year, though it *may*, if you blast it often with fertilizer. The lotus is a hardy plant, though, so if you successfully overwinter it indoors or out, it is sure to put on quite a show its second season in your water garden.

1. PREPARE THE TUBER. A lotus tuber, which looks a bit like a thin banana, is extremely fragile and brittle, and must be handled with great care. If you accidentally break off the growing end, you might as well throw the whole thing away, as the remaining section will rot anyway.

If your new lotus tuber has leaves intact, let them be unless they look poorly. Trim off any little roots that are crushed or dead. Keep the plant moist by submerging it in a bowl or tub of lukewarm water while you prepare its new home.

2. PREPARE THE CONTAINER. The larger the container, the better. For regular lotuses, this means a big tub of 20 to 32 quarts (20 to 32L) capacity; the dwarf kinds can be grown in something smaller, such as a 16-quarter (16L).

As for waterlilies, fill the container with heavy garden soil, but make certain it does not contain any manure, which can burn the fragile, fussy tuber. A high clay content is fine. Partially fill the container, adding fertilizer as described above.

3. POT THE PLANT. Use your finger to trace a little trough in the top of the soil. Gently lay the tuber horizontally into this trough. Cover the thickest part with an inch or two (2.5 to 5cm) of soil, but leave the growing tip exposed by about a half inch (12mm). Then, top off the pot with pea gravel or rocks (but no limestone, as lotuses are highly sensitive to its alkaline residue). If you're worried about the tuber floating away, place a heavier, flat

Above: This medley of moisture-loving plants includes broad-leaved water canna, grassy acorus, scarlet cardinal flowers, and 'Morden Pink' purple loosestrife.

stone above it. In any case, remember to leave the growing tip of the tuber exposed!

4. SET THE POT IN THE WATER. Lotuses prefer shallower water than do waterlilies. Start off the pot submerged by only an inch or two (2.5 to 5cm) of water, and gradually, over a period of a week or so, lower it to up to 4 inches (10cm). If necessary, use some bricks, a concrete block, or an empty, overturned pot to elevate the plant to the correct height.

DISPLAY DESIGN: COLOR

As with any part of your garden, giving thought to how plant colors work with one another in a water garden will lead to a prettier and more satisfying display. What is "successful" is really a matter of personal taste, but here are some ideas that have worked for other water gardeners:

● Use yellow as an accent. Most waterlilies have yellow centers (a flush of bright stamens). Placing an all-yellow waterlily next to one with, say, purple petals and yellow interior, makes for a dramatic display. You can grow yellow-blooming marginals and floaters for a variation on this effect. For example, water poppies (*Hydrocleys nymphoides*) have boldly shaped, buttery yellow flowers in enough profusion to call out the yellow in their neighbors.

● Make a composition in blue and purple. This may include any number of waterlilies, as well as some striking marginals such as certain irises, pickerel rush, and water hyacinth.

● Make a composition in blue and yellow. There are perhaps more waterlilies and marginals in these hues than any other colors. The combination always looks handsome, a natural harmony long favored by color theorists, from painters to gardeners.

● Monochromatic displays can be dramatic. A garden pool entirely of white, yellow, blue, or purple is easily achieved. To some eyes, this approach automatically gives a certain elegance to the display, and it draws attention to the many plant textures, forms, and habits.

● Make interesting foliage a pool feature. Water gardeners with fewer than eight hours of sun daily will be compelled to rely on the beauty of foliage, but it's not a bad idea in any event. Many marginals have fascinating foliage, from the four-lobed foliage of water clover to the variegated spears of some acorus and iris. Nonblooming plants such as horsetails benefit from being associated with such complementary companions as grassy-leaved cattails. The small, heart-shaped, red- or pink-splashed leaves of houttuynia are always fresh and pretty, weaving together the bolder leaves of waterlilies with the more delicate feathery foliage of parrot's feather. Many waterlilies feature pads with red or bronze markings that are attractive in their own right.

You don't want foliage types that are very similar too close together, as they can make for an uninteresting "forest" when out of bloom. Classic examples of this problem are irises paired with cattails (*Typha* species), pickerel rush (*Pontederia cordata*) with arrowhead (*Sagittaria*), and thalia (*Thalia*) with water canna (*Canna*).

Finally, make foliage color work with flower color. For instance, combine a yellow waterlily with the yellow-striped leaves of *Iris pseudacorus*. Try a purple-stemmed taro leaning over a purple-hued waterlily.

● Mix bold with bold, and delicate with delicate. You may not be able to pursue both of these tacks in one small pool or a tub garden. Wholeheartedly aiming for a theme can make for the most powerful display. Arrowhead, taro (*Colocasia*), and thalia are always stunning in the company of big tropical waterlilies or lotus. Plant scarlet water cannas or cardinal flowers with scarlet waterlilies, if you can get a match on the color; if not, combine two primary colors, such as red with yellow.

Softer-looking plants such as parrot's feather look lovely alongside the fringed flower petals of yellow or white water snowflake. Dwarf spike rush (*Eleocharis*) and dwarf cattail (*Typha minima*) look best in the company of smaller hardy waterlilies.

● Juxtapose a day-blooming waterlily with a night-bloomer. Overlapping bloom times create exciting possibilities. Generally speaking, day-bloomers close in the late afternoon, just as night-bloomers are beginning to unfurl. Bloom time may also overlap again the following morning, when the night-bloomer is still open and the day-bloomer is just starting a new day. By day, your pool could be a rainbow of various colors, evolving into an elegant, simpler garden of white and pink night-bloomers by evening.

● Especially if your pool is small, think carefully before closely mixing hardy and tropical waterlilies. The big flowers of the tropicals tend to rise up and overwhelm the smaller hardies, many of which float on the water's surface. As a result, the hardies may be lost to view altogether.

DISPLAY DESIGN: PLANT PLACEMENT

Once you've taken into account each plant's space and depth requirements, you are free to come up with attractive combinations. Again, successful mixtures are largely a matter of personal taste, but consider the following principles before setting the plants in place. Happily, because almost everything will be potted, you can always make adjustments later.

● Group like plants. A grouping of two, three, or more of each kind allows the plants to make a strong statement in the water garden. Using too many single individuals often leads to an overly busy display that lacks focus.

● Group plants according to height, bearing in mind the vantage from which the water garden will be viewed. Don't let imposing water cannas screen out graceful cattails, or allow the shorter white fairy wands of lizard's tail (*Saururus cernuus*) to be hidden by the taller, exuberant papyrus (*Cyperus*).

● Allow for a balance of the vertical and the horizontal. A pool planted exclusively with waterlilies, though lovely, can be more exciting with the introduction of some vertical-growing marginals. If your pool will accommodate only one waterlily and you want more horizontal interest, consider smaller, similar plants such as floating heart (*Nymphoides peltata*), water poppy (*Hydrocleys nymphoides*), or water snowflake (*Nymphoides cristata*), as well as floaters.

POOLSIDE LANDSCAPING

You'll want to disguise the pool's edge for practical reasons, to hide and protect the liner. But you'll also want to help your water garden fit into the rest of your landscape. Many water gardeners opt for the low-maintenance alternatives of hardscaping or grass at the pool's edge, and there's nothing wrong with that. If you install stonework or overlay with wooden decking, just remember to allow a stable lip to jut a bit out over the pool, as described in the previous chapter. If grass is your choice, try to plant it up as close to the pool edge as possible (first trim-

ming the liner as snugly as you dare). When laying sod, cut it into fairly small pieces, about a foot (30cm) long, so you can accommodate the pool's curves with as natural a curve as possible. Once it's all growing strong, you won't be able to tell where established lawn ended and new grass edging began.

Plants that arch, hang, or cascade are natural choices for the poolside because they soften the transition from lawn to water garden. Low-maintenance plants are best for this because they'll fill their roles quickly and leave you free to lavish attention on the water garden itself. Avoid plants that are prone to shedding a lot of foliage or flower petals, or you'll be cleaning up after them on the ground as well as in the adjacent water.

Moisture-lovers are popular—among them, candelabra primroses, irises, creeping jenny, and water mint—but don't

Above: This pink-tinged stone looks lovely against the backdrop of green plants and makes an attractive edging for a tiny water garden. Building the stone up into a series of rock shelves is an interesting option, and provides an important vertical dimension.

assume they'll enjoy a continual or adequate supply of damp soil there naturally. Supplemental water may be necessary, particularly if you live in a area with hot, dry summers. Place them far enough back from the edge that they'll be able to form adequate root systems and prosper. Potted plants, whether in attractive pots above ground, or sunk into the ground, are another option to consider.

Chapter 4

MAINTENANCE

Routine chores and special projects

Caring for a water garden in summer is not much different from attending to other parts of your garden. You'll fertilize, prune, ward off pests, and occasionally divide and repot. What you won't have to do, of course, is water. And for that reason alone, maintenance will feel less demanding—no rushing to hydrate flagging perennials on a hot day. In fact, water gardens positively adore hot summer days; waterlilies in particular will bloom with abandon.

As for the rest of the year, you'll have start-up and end-of-season chores, but nothing terribly taxing. Tried-and-true techniques for overwintering the plants, the creatures, and the pool itself are described in this chapter. You can keep your annual maintenance routine simple, or you may choose to get involved in a more elaborate regimen. Whatever you decide, you'll find the routine is basic and easy to follow.

Above: Russet and green royal ferns (*Osmunda regalis*) make a pretty autumn tapestry at pondside. Ferns are an excellent choice for pondside landscaping because they don't shed much debris into the water in autumn—a real cleanup problem with other plants.

Left: The advent of cold weather does not mean that your garden pool is dead for the year. Unless you expect the water to freeze solid, you may overwinter hardy plants, including hardy waterlilies, right in the pool. Like hardy perennials on land, they will simply go dormant.

SUMMER MAINTENANCE

CONTROLLING GROWTH Many lovely water plants are exuberant growers, which means that the water gardener spends less time coaxing and more time pruning. In wild ponds, plant life is kept in bounds by ducks and other waterfowl, and in some areas by muskrats and moose, too. Certain beetles and moths help. But you cannot count on the help of nature's pruners in a home water garden.

There are several tricks to keeping lusty plant growth in bounds, and you'd be wise to use them in combination when you can. First, plant everything in pots. Trim or hack back unwanted growth throughout the summer. If a plant seems to have unlimited energy, haul up its pot and check the roots to see whether it has exceeded its confines. Most aquatic plants can be divided even when growing and blooming at their peak, and suffer minimal trauma. Keep after the floating and underwater plants (you will learn to be vigilant if you find out the hard way that you added more than you should have). Otherwise, the pool will become as crowded as a swamp. Repot, give away, or discard the excess, or add it to your compost pile.

FERTILIZING Like all container-grown plants, aquatic plants in pots must be fed to thrive and bloom at their best. No matter how nutritious the garden loam you've placed them in may be, it won't be enough to support the continual, magnificent growth that makes a garden pool a showpiece. Fortunately, fertilizing water plants is easy and quick. Assuming you fed them at planting time, you need only give them another dose once a month throughout the season (two times a month is recommended if temperatures stay in the eighties for a prolonged period). If you forget, your plants will remind you. They'll produce fewer, and often smaller, leaves. The leaves may be lighter green or even yellow. And, they may stop flowering. Repotting can revive neglected plants, but what will really jump-start them is food. Cease fer-

Above: Many water gardeners cherish the splendid variegated foliage of *Houttuynia cordata*. While this plant may become an invasive pest in moist soil on land, grown in a submerged pot in a water garden, it is perfectly manageable and always a real asset.

Opposite: When the cool air and water temperatures of autumn arrive, growth begins to slow in the garden pool. Stop fertilizing your hardy waterlilies, and allow them to go dormant naturally. They can tolerate a frost or two. Then, haul them out of the water and prepare them for the coming winter, either in the pool itself (if it does not freeze solid) or indoors.

tilizing when autumn approaches, that is, several weeks before the first expected frost, so plant growth will slow down naturally for the coming winter.

Formulations low in nitrogen (N) and high in phosphorus (P) and potassium (K) are best. These favor flowers over foliage, and encourage healthier-looking plants overall. Water garden suppliers sell handy tablets, but you can use any number of other products, or a homegrown food. See "A Menu for Water Garden Plants" on the page opposite, for options. Smaller plants can be given smaller doses; it's easy to break a fertilizer tablet in half.

To fertilize, you may have to lean carefully out over the water, or even don shorts or waders and climb into the pool. Be careful you don't knock the pots off any supports they may be perched on, and try not to disturb the layer of pebbles or gravel you laid down on the potting soil surface at planting time, or you'll muddy the water—not the end of the world, but a temporary annoyance. Waterlilies and marginal plants do not have sensitive roots, so you can simply poke the fertilizer of your choice down into their pot's soil. Lotus roots, on the other hand, are so delicate that you'd best take extra care with the operation.

If Your Plants Don't Bloom

● They may not be getting enough sun. Prune nearby overhanging trees and shrubs if they cast shade on your pool. Trim back overenthusiastic aquatic neighbors.

● Feed your plants. Water garden plants respond quickly to a dose of fertilizer.

● Divide them. When aquatic plants are crowded, the little plantlets compete with each other and nobody really prospers. Repot in as many additional pots as necessary, or discard extras. Also, waterlilies that are rootbound don't bloom well and benefit from dividing and repotting.

PRUNING Regular pruning keeps your plants looking attractive, and it's also good for the pool. Without pruning, the water surface becomes overcrowded with foliage, and remember that a two-thirds coverage is optimum for shading the pool. If you allow leaves and flower stalks to yellow, wither, and drop on their own, they'll decay, and harmful, foul-smelling gases will build up in the water.

Trimming away spent flowers ("deadheading") from waterlilies and marginals is a good habit to develop. Aside from the practical reasons mentioned above, it inspires the plants to produce more flowers by frustrating their ability to go to seed, a process that can exhaust a plant. If the plant is prevented from producing seed, it will often continue to bloom in an effort to do so. Plus, if you let your aquatics produce seed, you may end up with an overpopulation problem on your hands.

Remove overgrown or yellowing leaves and spent flower stalks at their base. The outer leaves tend to be the older leaves, so removing them favors the new growth emerging from the plant's crown. Just snap them off with your fingers, or use sharp clippers. (Whatever you do, don't yank at the stems, or you may find yourself with a fistful of unpotted plant.) Toss the discards onto your compost pile, or dig them directly into a flower border or vegetable garden for mulch; aquatic plants break down quickly.

WATER LOSS: TOPPING OFF Your water garden will lose water to evaporation, and most rapidly during hot spells. Keep an eye on the situation and intervene when the level drops more than an inch (2.5cm); you'll see the high-water line on the side of your pool. Use a garden hose and gently trickle the water in. Never lower the hose into the pond—the water won't get aerated and the low oxygen levels are bad for your fish, plus you might leave it too long and the pool will overflow. If you don't feel like standing there with the hose, try setting an overhead sprinkler close to the pool's edge, and running it at less than maximum capacity so the water softly rains down on the pool's surface. With either of these

A Menu for Water Garden Plants

A single dose of any of the following fertilizers supplies adequate food for one feeding for one waterlily. Use more for big plants in big pots; use less for smaller plants or marginals, or if fertilizing more often than monthly. Mix the food into the potting soil at planting time. Later, you can simply tuck, poke, or punch the food down into the pot, well past the gravel layer on the soil surface. If necessary, use a dibble or broom handle.

● Tablets: Available from water gardening suppliers, these are specially formulated to feed waterlilies and other aquatic plants. Usually a 10-14-8 analysis. Follow the dosage recommendations on the label.

● Time-release fertilizer: Agriform™ or Osmocote, 13-13-13 formulation. This eliminates the need for repeated fertilizing and so is favored by water gardeners who tend a large collection of plants. Wrap a few handfuls in cheesecloth, burlap, or newspaper.

● Conventional granular garden fertilizer: In 5-10-5, 5-10-10, and 10-6-4 formulations, these can certainly do the trick. Wrap a few handfuls in cheesecloth, burlap, or newspaper. (Never use lawn food, which is too high in nitrogen and encourages leafy growth at the expense of bloom, plus it may include herbicides.)

● Blood meal: Wrap a handful in cheesecloth, burlap, or newspaper.

● A handful of well-rotted cow manure. Never use fresh manure, and use packaged manure only if it is well rotted, or you'll end up with murky water. Wrap in cheesecloth, burlap, or newspaper.

● Jobe's Fruit Tree Spikes™, a strong but slow-release 10-15-15 formulation, broken into walnut-size pieces.

Note: The phosphate (P) in chemical fertilizers may harm fish. To play it safe, supply phosphorus to your aquatics with bone meal instead.

methods, plants are not disturbed, and the pool adjusts gradually to the addition of water of a different temperature. Chlorine present in the added water should not pose a problem for the pool, and it will evaporate in a day or so. (Interestingly, studies have shown that such a small amount may have some value as a fungicide and algicide.)

If you find you need to add more than a few inches (7cm or so), additional chlorine may present a problem, particularly for the fish population. Also, a sudden dose of cold water can shock your tropical waterlilies into premature dormancy, and your hardies may be deformed. So if more than a few inches (7cm or so) of water are needed, either top off the pool as above several times over the course of several days, which will allow the pool to adjust slowly to each addition, or reserve sufficient water in buckets and wait a couple days before carefully pouring the water into the pool.

AUTUMN MAINTENANCE
LET THE PLANTS SLOW DOWN In early autumn, stop fertilizing your lilies and watch for signs of dormancy. The plants will stop flowering and producing new leaves; older leaves will turn yellow and die. Keep the plants in the pool until there has been a frost. The dying foliage will continue to feed the rootstocks, while the increasingly cool water will encourage the plants to go dormant. Once the water temperature drops to 50°F (10°C), remove the plants to prepare them for winter. Hardy plants can stay outdoors, though they'll need a little attention first; tropicals will have to spend the winter indoors.

LET THE FISH SLOW DOWN When cool weather comes, begin reducing and then withholding fish food. Your fish

will become less active, eventually retreating to the deepest part of the pool to wait out the winter in a state not unlike hibernation, in which their metabolism slows to an all-time low. Take care not to disturb them. If your pool freezes to the bottom, or if you fear it might, you'll have to remove the fish and overwin-ter them indoors in an aquarium. Catching all of the fish may be rather tricky, even if you're quick with the net. Your best bet may be to haul them up in early autumn before they retreat to the depths of the pool. For more details on general fish care, see Fish Matters, page 121.

Above: A pool and its inhabitants will get through a cold, snowy winter just fine. Your only concern should be that the surface never ice over completely, or harmful gases will build up. If it looks like ice will form, there are a number of things you can do to keep your pool "open." You can float a log on the surface, periodically poke through ice with a stick, or even invest in a stock-tank heater (the kind ranchers use to keep cattle water troughs from freezing over).

Opposite: There's no reason why your fish can't survive the winter in the pool. Help them prepare by reducing the amount you feed them in the autumn, and switching to a high-carbohydrate food so they can build up fat reserves. Eventually, they'll retreat to the muck at the bottom and enter a hibernationlike state.

WINTER CHECKLIST

PREPARE THE HARDY PLANTS FOR WINTER In all but the shallowest pools and the coldest climates, hardy plants can spend the winter outdoors with just a little preparation. After the first frost, haul them out of the water; take care not to hurt your back, as saturated pots can be heavy. Then, work on them at the poolside or, if it's too chilly outdoors, in a garage, greenhouse, or other workspace. If you wish, make fresh plant labels and poke them deep into each pot so you'll remember all the names come next spring. Chop off and discard all the leaves to within an inch (2.5cm) of the plant's crown (spare any tiny leaflets you see emerging from the crowns, as this is the beginning of next season's growth). Replenish the topping of gravel if necessary. Return the pots to the pool, placing them in the deepest part, where they are least likely to freeze or suffer from temperature fluctuations.

If your pool freezes clear to the bottom (or if you fear it might), you can easily overwinter the plants indoors. After their "haircut," top off the pots with a handful of straw, and store them in a dark, cool—but not freezing—place such as the garage or basement. Alternatively, remove the rhizomes from their pots, strip them of all remaining roots and foliage, and store each one in its own tightly sealed bag or jar of damp peat moss, in a cool, dark place. Don't forget to label!

Even if you have been meticulous, some plants probably will not survive the winter, for reasons ranging from the individual plant's health to exposure to freezing temperatures. But you can expect many of your overwintered plants to live to bloom again next summer.

OVERWINTER TENDER PLANTS Tropical waterlilies and marginals will not survive the winter outdoors in most parts of North America. Some water gardeners find it simplest to haul them out on autumn cleanup day and discard them, saving the pots for reuse, and buy new plants the next year. Others consider this waste-

Above: Overwinter treasured tender water garden plants indoors in a holding tank of warm water. A temperature of up to 75°F (24°C) is best, and can be achieved with an aquarium heater (available at pet stores that sell fish or in the catalogs of water garden suppliers). Check on them regularly and remove plants or plant parts that rot or die back.

≈≈≈

Opposite: Winter is a quiet time for a garden pool, but its life has not completely ceased. The water still needs to exchange oxygen with the air, which is why you shouldn't let the surface freeze over completely. If you visit the pool to see to this, take care not to stir up the pool bottom. Fish overwintering there might be disturbed and end up expending valuable energy, plus dormant plants may be adversely affected by chilly water from the upper layers of the pool.

ful (at $20 to $30 or more each, tropical waterlilies make expensive annuals), and opt to save and store the plants indoors.

There are two ways to store tropical waterlilies for the winter. The low-tech method is to strip the plants down to tubers and store them in damp builder's sand. After you haul the pots out of the pool for the year, gently tap each plant out of its pot and rinse off as much dirt as possible. Let it air-dry for a few days. Then snap or cut off any remaining leaves and flower stems.

Now examine the area just below the crown for the smooth, black, grape- to walnut-size tuber. Potbound specimens may have produced additional tubers. If you find several tubers, save the smaller ones, the "babies"; the "mother tuber" has likely exhausted her reserves and can be discarded. Gently separate the tubers from the crown and float them in tepid water for a day or so. Viable ones will sink and spoiled ones will float. Discard the spoiled ones. To ensure complete dormancy, some experts advise leaving the viable tubers in water for up to two weeks, rinsing them daily. Other suggest air-drying them for a few days in a cool room. Both techniques work well.

Keep the tubers in cool, damp builder's sand all winter. If the sand is too wet, the tubers will rot; too dry, and they will dehydrate. To get the right balance, fill a perforated container with sand, saturate it, and leave it to drain for a day. Then place some of the sand in a glass jar or plastic bag, set in a tuber, top it with more damp sand, and seal and label. Store the jar or bag in a cool (55°F [13°C]) spot where the tubers will not freeze. An unheated room in your house is probably your best bet.

The other method of overwintering tropical waterlilies and tropical marginals is to keep them going all winter in an indoor aquarium. You will have to maintain a fairly high water temperature, at least 75°F (24°C), and provide fluorescent lighting. The best place for such a setup is a good-size, heated greenhouse, though there are water gardeners who have successfully converted a room or a basement to this use.

PREPARE THE POOL FOR WINTER For gardeners in areas with cold and snowy winters, the main worry is the formation of ice on the surface of the pool, or worse, that the pool will freeze solid. If this is a concern for you, the first thing to do is lower the water level from several inches (10cm or so) to a foot (30cm) to allow for expanding ice.

A layer of ice on the surface of your pool is bad news. For starters, it prevents the healthy and necessary exchange of gases between the atmosphere and the water. Organic matter trapped in the water will break down and produce foul-smelling toxic gases (ammonia, hydrogen sulfide, and excessive carbon dioxide). Also, an ice layer traps snow on its surface, and even a thin layer prevents sunlight from getting to any plants left to overwinter below.

Fortunately, there are many easy ways to keep the ice layer from becoming a problem. (If you're not expecting ice to be a constant problem, intervene on those mornings when you spot a layer developing on the surface of the pool.) The most low-tech option, and one that works well for many water gardeners, is to float a piece of firewood or a chunk of scrapwood in the pool. Alternatively, poke in a branch or pole of some kind, and trek out to the water garden every few days to jiggle it. Or set a hot kettle or pan of hot water on the ice to melt it.

An increasingly popular mechanical solution to the ice problem is to invest in a stock-tank heater, the kind farmers and ranchers use to keep livestock water troughs free of ice in the winter months. A perfectly acceptable model will run you only about $50. These come equipped with a thermostat, and switch on when the water temperature drops below freezing.

If your pool has a recirculating pump or fountain, you might be tempted to use it to keep water moving all winter, and thus prevent ice from forming, or at least from forming a permanent cover. While a recirculating pump or fountain will keep the oxygen moving, it may also send chilly water down to the pool bottom, disturbing and perhaps harming your fish or plants there.

Fountains, waterfalls, and biological filters should all be turned off during freezing weather.

Finally, you could cover most, but not all, of your pool with some sort of insulating material. Some water gardeners use foam house insulation with good results. Of course, the best insulator is snow. It is critical to make sure there's a spot open for air exchange.

MILD-CLIMATE WINTERIZING Most, if not all, aquatic plants and fish can remain in the pool year-round in milder climates, but autumn cleanup is nonetheless useful. If you're at all concerned about the most tender plants or most precious tropical waterlilies, take them out and carry them through the winter using the methods described above. Or construct a simple plastic tent over the pool and let heat escape on days when it's warm enough for an excessive buildup of heat. Some water gardeners cut slits in the plastic to let heat out.

If ice appears on the pool surface, take care of it immediately, first thing in the morning. You don't have to break it up—just create a small opening so any toxic gases that may have built up can escape. Whatever you do, don't whack the ice, because the shock waves can kill your fish.

EARLY SPRING: A FRESH START

INVENTORY When the first water gardening catalogs arrive early in the year, it's time to start thinking about and planning for the coming summer. Pay a visit to any plants you've stored to make sure they have fared well. Discard rhizomes and tubers that show signs of mold or rot. Brush the straw off the surface of the sheared, potted plants and nudge around for signs of life. But don't make hasty decisions about viability; a plant that looks dead is probably still dormant.

Consult your memory (or gardening notebook, if you have one), and check your store of supplies. Place your orders with mail-order firms early. They are apt to run out of popular plants.

Don't worry about when they will ship your plants; they monitor the weather and temperatures nationwide, and won't ship until it's the right planting time in your hardiness zone.

REVIVE TROPICAL WATERLILY TUBERS
About a month before your last expected frost date, check the tubers to see if sprouts have emerged. If they haven't, place the tubers in water on a sunny windowsill to get them going. Pot sprouted tubers temporarily in 5- or 6-inch (12 to 15cm) pots, setting them a quarter-inch (6mm) deep in heavy garden topsoil (heavy, so it won't float away once the pot is in water). Top the pot with pebbles or gravel and stick in a label.

To keep the plants moist, set them in an aquarium or large pail with about 3 inches (7.5cm) of water over the rims of the pots. The water should be 70 to 80°F (21 to 27°C); you'll probably have to use an aquarium heater to maintain this temperature. You'll also want to shine fluorescent lights or grow lights. In two to six weeks, when new leaves make their debut, move the plants into bright sunlight.

Leave the little plants in the small pots as long as possible. Tropical waterlilies must not be moved into the pool outdoors until the pool water temperature has climbed into the mid-70s°F (mid-20s°C), which may not happen until June in some areas. If you are impatient and put them out in water that is too cold for them, they may be shocked back into dormancy, or suffer delayed growth and flowering.

On moving day, transplant each one into a large pot. Then place it at the proper depth in the pool (no more than 6 to 8 inches (15 to 20cm) deep, supported on overturned pots, bricks, or blocks. And look forward to another summer of blossoms. You'll be amazed and gratified by how fast overwintered lilies grow into mature plants.

REVIVE HARDY WATERLILIES For the plants you've left in the pool over the winter: one fine day in spring, when the water temperature is in the 50s°F (10s°C), don your waders and retrieve the pots. Haul them out of the pool and examine the plants for signs of life; they should be breaking dormancy. Remove bedraggled foliage that may be just hanging on. Then, poke in some fertilizer, and top off the pot with a fresh layer of pebbles if needed. Return the pots to the pool, immersing them no more than 6 to 8 inches (15 to 20cm) deep.

Unlike their tropical cousins, hardy waterlilies will not be traumatized by cool water. They can be set out in water that has reached 50°F (10°C) or more. Hardy waterlilies will acclimate, and slowly but surely come back to life as the water and air warm.

If you stored some pots of hardies in a cool place indoors over the winter, retrieve them when they begin to show signs of life. Fertilize, and top off with pebbles. Then take them outdoors and give them a good soaking with the hose (taking care not to wash away their soil). After excess water has drained away, return them to the pool. If you've stored the rhizomes in bags or jars of peat moss, wait until conditions seem right outdoors, then rescue them and pot them up. Then, follow the same steps for getting them back into the pool.

DIVIDE HARDY WATER PLANTS

Spring is the perfect time to increase your stock. Rootstocks will not be traumatized by the operation; instead, they'll burst into vigorous new growth. Examine hardy waterlily rhizomes carefully for growing tips and, using a sharp knife, cut them into chunks that have one or more each. The same goes for water iris rhizomes. It may take more than a sharp knife to divide some hardy marginals, particularly if they are rootbound. The sharp blade of a trowel may do the trick, or try a machete or similar tool. Make sure every section you pot up displays a good clump of viable (white, not black or limp) roots.

Repot according to the directions in the previous chapter. Don't forget to fertilize and, if you wish, label. Hardy aquatics can go right into the pool—at the proper depths—when the water has reached at least 50°F (10°C).

FISH IN SPRING

The warmer water of spring will gradually awaken fish that have overwintered on the bottom of the pool. When you spot them darting about, resist the temptation to feed them. Like the plants, they are gradually coming back to life, and if you feed them too soon, they may not be able to digest properly. They can get by for the first few weeks on algae. Reintroduce food gradually, and watch to see that they actually eat it.

If you've lost some fish over the winter, or want to add more, now is the time to restock. To introduce fish to your pool for the first time, always float them in a plastic bag of water on the pool surface for a few hours before releasing them, so they can adjust to the temperature. Don't let the bag drift into a patch of hot sunlight; if you're concerned about the danger of overheating, drape a towel over the bag. For more information on caring for fish, see Fish Matters, page 121.

ADDING NEW PLANTS TO THE POOL

Follow the directions in Chapter Three, Stocking and Planting, for detailed information on potting, fertilizing, and positioning water plants and marginals. Add them to the pool only when you are sure the water is warm enough: 50°F (10°C) or warmer for hardy waterlilies and hardy marginals; 70°F (21°C) or warmer for tropical waterlilies, tropical marginals, oxygenators, and floating plants.

THE BIG CLEANUP: WHEN AND HOW TO DRAIN AND CLEAN THE WHOLE THING

A water garden that enjoys regular maintenance does not need to be drained and refilled. If it has a proper balance of plants and creatures, and has reached a state of equilibrium where algae is not out of control (though it may be present), leave well enough alone. Introducing a fresh batch of water returns the pool to "square one." It may take weeks or even months for it to return to a state of balance.

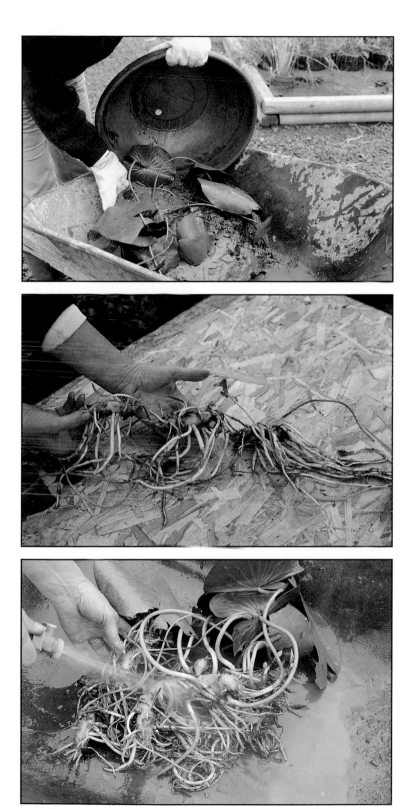

1. It's easy to divide your waterlilies. Begin by dumping the root ball out of the pot (watch that you don't hurt your back—full pots full of saturated soil can be surprisingly heavy). Handle the plant gently so you don't damage it.

2. Now, carefully wash the soil away and inspect the plant's roots. Viable roots are crisp and white. Trim away any that arc broken or black.

3. Examine the rootstock for "eyes" or growing tips. Using a clean, sharp knife, cut the rootstock into sections, each with an eye and some healthy roots. Repot each one, and expect a bounty of new plants.

However, there may be times when this onerous chore is necessary. The most common reason is to remove organic debris built up thickly on the bottom. In the case of some water gardens, this means a drain-and-refill every other year; for others, only every third or fourth year is necessary. You should intervene, regardless of the timing, if the water doesn't clear and appears to be getting worse, or if the pool develops an ongoing problem with oily scum on the surface (this is often accompanied by an unpleasant smell). If you've decided to go ahead, try to wait for dry weather. If the soil surrounding the pool is saturated, from spring or autumn rains, it may cave in on the empty liner, or pop the liner out of the ground, because an empty pool doesn't exert any pressure on the surrounding soil.

Remove all the contents of the pool before draining, of course. Potted plants will manage for a short time out of water, but keep them shaded to minimize stress. If in doubt, have buckets and other containers on hand to hold the plants while you work. Catch as many fish and snails as you can—you are sure to come across a few you've missed as the water level lowers. Hold them in buckets of *pool* water. Segregate them in separate buckets so they'll all get enough oxygen...and so they don't discover easy meals in the confined space!

You can bail out the water, use a hose or hoses to siphon, or, if you have one, let your submersible pump do the work for you. Don't divert the water into the street, as this is often illegal. Besides, pool water is full of organic matter that the rest of your garden will relish. Dump it on flower or shrub beds, or use it to water the vegetable garden or lawn. Save and toss back in healthy pieces of floating plants so they can rejuvenate when you refill the pool.

Once the water is out, you may be tempted to give the liner a good scrubbing. Don't. Leave some algae on the sides. Scoop out or sweep out excessive silt on the bottom, but leave a little. Over time, beneficial bacteria have established themselves there, and it's unwise to remove them. Now you can refill the pool. Let the water stand for a few days so the remaining silt will settle back on the bottom, the chlorine can dissipate, and the water can warm up. In the meantime, check on the reserved water plants daily to make sure they are not suffering. Give the fish and snails a little food or a handful of duckweed. Reintroduce them gradually by letting their holding-container water mix with the new pond water; they'll swim out into their new home when they're ready.

TROUBLESHOOTING: COMMON PROBLEMS AND THEIR SOLUTIONS

Generally speaking, a healthy pool is a happy pool. Plants that are well cared for, in a pool that has achieved a state of balance, are less likely to suffer from pests and diseases. Stress—such as insufficient sunlight, a shocking addition of a quantity of cold water, or not enough fertilizer—makes plants more vulnerable. So even if you are able to combat or treat successfully one of the problems described below, you should also take a look at the overall state of your water garden and make adjustments where you can to make sure all its residents are as healthy as possible.

APHIDS A common pest in some water gardens, the aphid favors lilypads and the foliage of some marginals, especially irises. Crowds of tiny, busy white or black sucking insects appear here and there. If unchecked, they soon coat their victims, thanks to their voracious appetite and fast reproduction. They can literally drain the life out of your plants.

Fortunately, aphids are easy to fight if you catch them in the act early. You can remove and discard affected leaves. If that would mean removing too many leaves, blast the aphids off the leaves with a fairly forceful spray of water, or push the leaves underwater and swish them around. The pests will lose their grasp, at least temporarily—and if your fish aren't overfed, they'll quickly be gobbled up.

In cold-winter climates, freezing temperatures will kill aphids. In mild climates, aphids can become an ongoing problem, overwintering on the plants (check carefully in the leaf nodes, where they can hide). As winter is a slow time for your pool anyway, you might as well prune out all affected leaves; new, unaffected growth will appear in spring. Research has shown that aphids in mild climates also overwinter on plum and cherry trees, so if you have some of those in your yard, you might try breaking the cycle by spraying them with a dormant oil, applied according to label directions. This will be effective, of course, only if there are no plum or cherry trees in your neighbors' yards; if there are, perhaps you can persuade them to spray, or offer to do it for them.

CHINA MARK MOTH LARVAE China Mark moth (*Hydrocampa* species) larvae get their start in the water garden when the adult moths lay their eggs on the undersides of waterlily pads. They hatch as small green or yellowish leaf-cutting larvae. They aren't actually dining on the leaves (the chunks they nibble off are too large)—rather, they build themselves little floats that hide them from predators, and travel about the pool dining on small bits of organic matter. When the larvae are ready to pupate, they drill a hole down into a waterlily leaf stem, and emerge later as adult moths, completing their life cycle. Meanwhile, the affected leaf will suffer from this intrusion, turning limp or yellow and, eventually, dying.

Your best defense is to catch them early, before the deposited eggs hatch, by wiping off the bottoms of the lilypads on a regular basis during the summer months. If you discover the actual larvae themselves, handpick and dispose of them far from the pool.

CROWN ROT Crown rot is a highly contagious disease of waterlily rootstocks. Early signs include rotting, black stems; buds that never quite make it to the water surface, turning black, rotting, and falling away; pads that start out fine but for no apparent reason turn yellow and die after a few days; and an odd smell. Close inspection may reveal an alarming sight: the tuber or rhizome may be immersed in a gelatinous, foul-smelling goo.

Act immediately, removing the affected plants. Take the roots out of the pot, spray them off with the hose or dunk them in a bucket of water, then examine them. If they are rotten through and through, you have no choice but to discard the plant. If there appear to be some healthy sections, chop out and discard the affected portions, repot the plant in fresh soil, and hope for the best. (Wash out and disinfect the pot with a mild bleach solution first, or use a new pot.)

Research suggests that waterlilies with mottled foliage, especially those in the yellow-to-orange range, are most susceptible. In any case, you can prevent the problem ahead of time by soaking newly arrived plants overnight in a bucket of water to which you've added a few drops of liquid fungicide.

HAIL Hail is a byproduct of summertime thunderstorms, when precipitation high in the atmosphere forms into small, roundish lumps of ice during its descent. It usually comes up suddenly and finishes suddenly, but even a brief shower of hail can create havoc in a water garden. The relatively thin, horizontal lilypads are especially vulnerable, and hail can shred or perforate them. There's little you can do except prune off the damage and wait for the plants to rebound...which won't take long!

LEAF SPOT Little brown spots on the leaves, or browned edges, are usually signs that your plants are suffering from a fungal problem. Not surprisingly, they usually appear when the weather has been especially hot and humid and the air stiflingly still. They can also appear after prolonged rainy spells. Remove and discard all affected foliage from the plant's crown. The plants will soon generate replacement leaves.

ANIMAL PESTS

Unfortunately, water gardens aren't enticing to us alone. They're irresistible to a number of animals, not all of them welcome. In the case of wild animals, they may be drawn to our yards because their own habitat is shrinking. Trapping and releasing these unwelcome visitors in a faraway part of town or swampy area is now illegal in many areas, as is killing them with poison or a gun.

As in coping with pests in other parts of your garden, sometimes a balance can be struck. You may be able to tolerate the presence of an occasional visitor without going to war. But if an uninvited animal becomes a major threat to the beauty and health of your water garden, there are steps you can take to discourage it. Admittedly, some of these techniques are homegrown, but they may well work for you.

Bear in mind that most unwelcome visitors are waders, not swimmers. A shelf on the side of the pool is a wonderful platform from which to fish, nibble on plants, or step down into the depths of the pool. So the first obvious defense is to keep lots of potted plants on these shelves, allowing no corridor or opening. You should also keep the pool full of plants, so maneuvering around in it looks like more trouble than it's worth (remember, two-thirds coverage of the water's surface is ideal). If you get desperate, you can spread a thin net or grate across the entire pool, anchoring it firmly to the banks, but it's not easy to make this shield attractive.

HERONS Of all the birds drawn to water gardens, herons are the most destructive. Most common are blue herons. They tend to travel alone and must have excellent eyesight, because they can zero in on even a small water garden. They immediately set to dining on your fish and can empty an entire pool in short order.

To discourage them, you need to use their behavior patterns against them. You'll notice they never land right on the water but rather on the ground. They walk over to the pool's edge and work from there, or step down onto the ledge or even wade all the way in. Their long legs and long, sharp beaks make them fast, versatile fishermen. If herons are a problem for you, you must keep them from the pool's edge. A barrier of plants alone doesn't seem to deter them. A method that really works is to place short stakes (6 inches [15cm] or so tall) around the pool, and string clear fish-

Opposite: Though pretty, ducks can be real pests in a water garden. Unlike some birds, they won't eat your fish, but they will eat or damage your plants and foul the water with their droppings.

ing line between them. As it approaches the pool, the heron will bang its legs against this barrier; though it won't hurt him, it will stop the heron in his tracks. He may retreat and try to approach from another angle, so it's important to protect the whole perimeter. After a few attempts, he'll give up in disgust.

Another method some water gardeners employ with at least temporary success is placing an artificial heron near the pool, a sort of decoy in reverse. Because herons are territorial, the theory goes that they'll see that your pool is already "taken" and pass it by. You'll need to move the false heron around from time to time so any real heron that may be watching doesn't begin to suspect the truth.

The decoy and "scare" balloons sometimes used by gardeners to keep crows away from their corn plants may also be worth a shot, though they certainly won't do much for the water garden's appearance.

DUCKS AND GEESE You wouldn't think these birds would be interested in smaller garden pools, simply because the size doesn't promise good dining or swimming possibilities. Wrong. The only good news is that if ducks or geese do appear, they won't go after your fish. Unfortunately, they like aquatic plants, especially the submerged ones and newly planted lilies, and will sometimes eat pieces out of the leaves of mature lilies. Their droppings can become a problem in the pool (excess organic material leads to algal blooms) as well as in your landscape (an unsightly mess). They may also carry diseases that will transfer to your fish population.

Fortunately, ducks and geese aren't as difficult as herons to dissuade. Plantings close by the pool's edge are sufficient to discourage them, as is a water surface given over to the maximum coverage by waterlily pads. Ducks and geese are shy of dogs and humans, and can also be frightened away with scare balloons, decoy animals, and noise-making repellents.

RACCOONS These pests adore water. An increasing problem in urban and suburban areas, they survive on trash-picking and may discover your water garden quite by accident. Raccoons may come to your pool to wash their food, and they may stay when they notice the delicious array of fish laid at their feet. They're expert fishermen, but they aren't very graceful, which means that in their zeal for their meal, they'll knock over pots or nudge out roots and plant tags. Ironically, racoons will sometimes kill the fish but not eat them.

To discourage raccoons, try a forest of marginals at the pool's edge to make it difficult for them to wade in. Provide your fish with plenty of hiding places by growing as many waterlilies as your pool can hold. Don't add any crawfish—raccoons find them absolutely irresistible.

There is a virtual arsenal of anti-raccoon war tactics, which may or may not work for you; you may want to use them in combination or in sequence. You could try frightening the raccoons away using one of the light or sound alarms that some vegetable gardeners use. Or place a battery-operated radio, set to an all-news station, near the pool. The presence of a dog on the grounds is effective, assuming the pet will not be too cold to spend time outdoors *and* won't wake up the entire neighborhood announcing his displeasure with the visitors. A different, rather interesting tack is to provide a more accessible meal for the raccoons, such as a nearby dish of cat food (though there is a story of a water gardener who caught a clever raccoon in the act of dropping bits of cat food into the water as bait to lure the fish over to the pool's edge, where he snatched them up!). Finally, consider repellents. Sprinkle blood

meal around the edge of the pool and replenish it periodically. Apparently raccoons abhor the smell. Fox urine is also said to be very effective in repelling them, but where in the world are you going to get that?

MUSKRATS Muskrats can be a problem if a wild wetland, pond, or stream is nearby. They like to dine on arrowhead, cattails, grasses, reeds, and sedges, and they find waterlily and canna rootstocks a gourmet treat. Like raccoons, they are clumsy in the small world of a garden pool and will knock over or unpot plants. Also, their sharp claws can slash a liner. One visit, and your water garden will be a real mess. Try the tactics listed above for repelling raccoons. You may need to limit the number of grassy-leaved marginals in your pool to make it less tempting. If worse comes to worst, erect a small, low fence around your pool.

TURTLES These creatures rarely appear in numbers and can be unobtrusive, adding "character" to your water garden. For the most part, turtles are vegetarians and just one is unlikely to do much damage. However, if you notice your waterlilies are being nibbled on more than you'd like or if there's a drop in your fish population, you'll know whom to suspect.

The only remedy is to trap the culprit and return him to the nearby marsh or stream whence he probably came and hope he stays away. Netting a turtle is easier said than done, however. They are not as slow moving as children's stories would have you believe—when in the water. Your best bet is to snag a turtle when he is sunning himself, usually in the morning. (Turtles are cold-blooded and must sit out in the sun to raise their body temperature.)

If your problem turtle is the fearsome snapping turtle, be cautious. If you're strong and brave, handle him by a back leg to avoid the reach of his jaws. To trap him in the water, use oily canned sardines or a piece of chicken liver as bait. If the project is too daunting, call your local animal control officer or fish and wildlife service for help.

CATS Domestic cats are enthralled by water gardens, but don't seem to be as willing as wild animals to climb in after the fish. A cat is more likely to just sit watching at the pool's edge for hours. Take care not to startle him, though, or he may take a tumble into the water; this is most likely to happen in the case of a container garden, where the fascinated cat may keep a precarious perch on the rim.

If you suspect a cat is fishing and want to discourage him, there are a host of possible remedies, among them spreading mothballs, or pouring liquid from boiled onions or tobacco tea (made from steeping cigarettes in water), around the pool. Some garden centers and catalogs sell cat repellents that may be worth a try. In all cases, you'll have to replenish the repellent after a rain.

A tried-and-true method for keeping cats out of flower beds will work well in a water garden setting too, so long as your poolside landscaping does not prohibit it. Lay lengths of poultry wire around the edge of the pool, projecting out about a foot on all sides. If this area is not given over to grass, you may be able to hide the wire from view with a thin layer of soil. When a cat walks on it or tries to dig, his paws get snagged and he decides to go elsewhere.

WHEN YOUR POOL IS DAMAGED

Suspect your liner is damaged when the water level drops very quickly and without warning. A pool liner can sustain damage in various ways: from the sharp nails of a marauding animal, a string trimmer or lawn mower that strayed too close, or the natural decomposition process that occurs when plastic has been exposed to direct sunlight for too long.

To get a good look at the problem, lower the water level gradually until you locate the damaged area, then stop. If it's a minor leak, you can patch it. If you find extensive tearing or cracking, it's time to replace your liner. Proper preventive measures will save a lot of time, effort, money, and heartache. Edge your pool when you install it, and repair it immediately when necessary. Also, keep the pool well filled and don't procrastinate in warding off animal pests. These steps will go a long way toward prolonging the life of your liner.

PATCHING To get the longest possible life out of a patch, obey the following instructions to the letter. First, do the repair on a warm, sunny day when the liner will be most flexible. Scrub the trouble spot clean of algae or other residue, and apply the patch only when it is totally dry. Pinholes and small nicks can be covered with a dab of neoprene paint or adhesive-backed tape, but larger cuts require a PVC patch. Patching kits are available from catalogs and garden centers that cater to water gardening. As you work, take care not to stretch the liner, or you'll weaken the result. Afterward, direct hot air from a blow dryer to ensure a tight seal and that the patch is snug. (Remember to be extra-cautious about running any electrical appliance near water—do not stand in or even touch the water while operating an electrical appliance!)

EXCESSIVE WATER LOSS If you are unfortunate enough to be away from home for some time when a leak occurs, don't panic on your return. All may not be lost, as nature has its own survival mechanisms. Take the plants out and prune off obviously dead foliage. You may notice that the stress caused them to jettison some leaves; this means new growth will be poised to take off when the plant recovers. You may also notice that algae coated the plants, staving off dehydration. Move the plants to containers of pool water or water that has sat long enough to let chlorine evaporate.

As for the fish and snails, they will have retreated to the area of most water or plant cover, to protect themselves from drying out. If the pool is really low, check the silt at the pool's bottom. Transfer survivors to a temporary home. You may lose a few more, but some may pull through. Then, clean out all dead plant debris and dead creatures before refilling the pool. Remember to let the newly filled pool sit empty for a day or longer while the chlorine evaporates, or to treat the water with a dechlorinator; then, get the survivors back in the pool as quickly as possible.

Chapter 5

PLANTS FOR THE WATER GARDEN

Overviews and selections

Plants for the water garden range widely in their form, habit, color, texture, and height, just like any other category of garden plants. You'll find that you have tremendous choice in planning for your water garden plants, from brightly colored waterlilies, both hardy and tropical, to fragrant, cup-shaped water lotuses to graceful sedges to free-floating water ferns.

Depending upon your tastes, the size of your pool or container, and the style of your water garden, you may decide on just a few select plants or you may want to include lots of different types. Potted aquatics, floaters, marginals, and bog-lovers for the poolside make a lush-looking water garden scene, as long as your pool is of adequate size. In the pages that follow, you'll find the basic cultural requirements for a variety of water plants, as well as descriptions of species and cultivars that are particularly desirable or easy to grow. No matter what your water garden theme or design, you're sure to find scores of beautiful options.

Above: The hardy striped manna grass *Glyceria maxima* 'Variegata' is a popular choice for water gardens because it forms a manageable, attractive clump no more than two feet (60cm) high.

Opposite: Individual waterlily blossoms remain in bloom for at least three days. Close inspection of the flower reveals that it changes during this period. The petals and sepals may change color, depending on the variety. And the stamens gradually close inward to form a tepee shape by the last day (interestingly, the bloom is considered female at first and male by the time the stamens close over).

WATERLILIES

Despite their exquisite beauty, waterlilies are by no means frail. With enough sun (six hours a day minimum) and proper care, they'll grow vigorously and bloom with abandon all summer long. Most keep civilized hours, opening in midmorning and closing in late afternoon. As Monet biographer Marc Elder so charmingly put it, "Like all beautiful people, the waterlilies rise late and even the sun has to come and beg them to." A few waterlilies in the tropical group bloom at night, or rather from late afternoon, through the night, and until midmorning the following day, mak-ing them the perfect choice for gardeners who are away at work or school all day.

Individual waterlily blossoms last for three or more days. Interestingly, they open female, stay that way for the first day only, then become male. You can tell what stage a flower is in by look-ing for the presence of sappy liquid in the middle; later on, the stamens close over it, forming a tepee shape. Bees adore waterlilies and are constantly browsing among them at all stages, so it's no surprise that they have been the agent of many a hybrid. (See "The Mysterious World of Waterlily Hybridizing, opposite.")

The Mysterious World of Waterlily Hybridizing

Bees love waterlilies, and the gardening world has welcomed many lovely hybrids thanks to accidental crossings. Purposeful crossings, on the other hand, have been both difficult to achieve and tricky to track or document. (No wonder waterlily nomenclature has been in disarray.) This seems to be because hybrids so rarely produce viable seed.

A great many beautiful lilies still popular today originated around the turn of the century in the nursery of a French breeder by the name of Joseph Bory Latour-Marliac. While his successes were obvious, his methods were not, and they have left modern breeders baffled and gnashing their teeth in frustration. The records he left behind have been called "misleading at best," the implication being that he did not wish anyone to follow in his footsteps. Bill Heritage, a British aquatic plant expert, has a slightly different theory. He suspects Marliac's secret "lay not in a special pollinating technique but in a deliberate policy of naming and releasing only hybrids he believed to be infertile." This, grants Heritage, could well have been public-spirited, to prevent unwanted seedlings from cropping up in water gardens.

Fertile seed is the would-be hybridizer's fondest wish. Then, if he can get the seeds to germinate, he can judge whether any of the new plants is a keeper. From there, it's a matter of vegetatively propagating the new variety (by dividing and growing on the rootstock) and building up stock.

One of Marliac's tricks was to use as one of the parents a species lily known to be fertile. Apparently he used several, both American and European. Modern-day hybridizers may or may not have rediscovered all his secrets, but they have had success using wild species waterlily such as *Nymphaea mexicana, N. alba, N. odorata,* and others. Experts can guess a plant's parentage or at least its characteristics by observing variations in the rootstocks that trace back to the species parents. At any rate, after a long interval, the 1970s, 1980s, and 1990s saw a flush of new waterlilies. Two outstanding breeders now dominate the field, Perry Slocum of North Carolina and Dr. Kirk Strawn of Texas. Two others are Ken Landon of Texas and Charles Winch of Australia.

If you'd like to try your hand at hybridizing, transfer pollen from a lily blossom in its second or later day of blooming to the liquid-filled center of a just-opened lily on another plant. Then, to protect your experiment from contamination by zealous bees, bag the lily in cheesecloth or an old stocking, label it, and let it sink. Seed will be trapped when the pod bursts open—generally, in about three weeks. Tropical lily seed can be dried. Hardy lily seed must be stored in water and kept in a refrigerator. The growing process requires patience, and you'll need a warm greenhouse, or at least heating cables under the seed flats. Assuming some of the seeds germinate, you need to let the plants grow to a size where you can evaluate the results. From start to finish, this can take several seasons. Sound like more trouble than it's worth? Perhaps this is why there aren't vast numbers of waterlily hybrids.

Waterlily names A worldwide register finally exists, under the sponsorship of the International Water Lily Society. Every major mail-order water garden supplier is a member and has pledged to use the master list. However, the register was a very long time coming, and it will take some time to straighten out all the years of mistakes and confusion. So if you buy a waterlily and it doesn't turn out to be quite what you expected in color or habit, go back to the supplier or try another nursery.

You'll notice that waterlilies are frequently named after a person, often a family member or friend of the hybridizer. It makes a well-stocked pool sound like the guest list at an IWLS symposium dinner. This is by no means intended as a slight to all the great people commemorated by a waterlily hybrid, but this trend in naming isn't helpful to new water gardeners. Such names offer nothing in the way of description (or, often, of charm). On the other hand, this situation forces us to judge a lily by its looks and catalog description, instead of being seduced into buying by an appealing, poetic name.

New varieties New plants make their debut every year, and we can expect this growth to accelerate in the coming years as hybridizers fine-tune their techniques, and as more hybridizers inevitably enter the field. A good place to view new introductions is in the displays of public gardens that have good aquatics collections, such as the Denver Botanic Garden and Longwood Gardens in Pennsylvania. Or visit your nearest water-gardening nursery.

Just because a plant is new doesn't mean it's for connoisseurs. Quite the contrary, in fact. Beginning water gardeners stand to benefit the most from advances in hybridization because new varieties may be a considerable improvement over plants that have been around a long time.

The Difference between Hardies and Tropicals

Hardy waterlilies:

- flowers float on the water surface (with a few exceptions, or when crowded)
- grow from a hardy, fleshy rhizome
- tend to have smaller flowers, 4 to 7 inches (10 to 18cm) across
- can survive a winter of freezing temperatures outdoors (so long as the root itself doesn't freeze)
- come in shades of red, white, pink, and yellow, and "changeables"
- feature leaf edges that are smooth

Tropical waterlilies:

- hold their blossoms several inches (up to 8 [20cm] or more) above the water's surface, and thus are easier to admire from a distance
- grow from a tender tuber
- tend to have larger blossoms, up to 12 inches (30cm) across, and are more fragrant
- cannot survive cold winters outdoors
- offer all the same colors as hardies, with the addition of magnificent blues and purples, and of night-bloomers
- feature leaf edges that are scalloped or toothed

WHAT DOES "VIVIPAROUS" MEAN? This term is used to describe waterlilies—tropical waterlilies only, to be exact—that produce new little "piggyback" plantlets at the center of their leaves. For most home water gardeners, this quality is merely a curiosity, though it's simple to harvest the plantlets and grow them into new plants. To do this, gently tear or cut away the big leaf from the plantlet and lay it (it may have tiny roots, or will soon develop them) on the surface of a flat of moist builder's sand and peat. Keep the flat warm and out of direct sunlight, keep the medium moist, and slowly but surely the new waterlily will grow. Later, when a tiny tuber is established, you can pot it up and add it to the water garden. The length of time this process takes varies wildly. The youngster will look exactly like its parent.

A NOTE ON WATERLILY HARDINESS As you would expect, hardy waterlilies are able to survive winter outdoors in colder climates, when properly prepared and lowered to the bottom of a pool that is deep enough. It is safe to say that most are hardy in Plant Hardiness Zones 4 or 5 to 10. Tropical waterlilies, on the other hand, may be left out for the winter only in Zones 9 and 10, during which time they'll continue blooming (though not as heavily, as you might expect). For overwintering instructions, see the previous chapter.

SELECTIONS There are dozens of choices in every category. Here are but a few of the widely available, easy-to-grow classics. They are good choices for beginners. Always take into account plant size (spread) when planning for your pool.

HARDY WATERLILIES
'Attraction'
Unique among waterlilies for its variable but gorgeous coloring, this plant has cup-shaped, semidouble flowers that are brushed with pink and white when young and eventually turn a deep garnet red with flecks of white. Adding to the drama are mahogany stamens. Large for a hardy, from 7 to 10 inches (18 to 25cm) across, they are sure to excite admiration from visitors to your garden. Spread: 6 feet (1.8m).

'Charlene Strawn'
A classic, easy-to-grow yellow waterlily, this one holds its star-shaped flowers slightly above the water surface in the manner of a tropical waterlily. Plus, it is fragrant. A wonderful choice for beginners. Spread: 6 to 12 feet (1.8 to 3.7m)

'Chromatella' (*Marliacea chromatella*)
This popular yellow waterlily has stood the test of time; it is one of the oldest hybrids, and has many excellent qualities. The beautiful cup-shaped flowers are laden with chiffon yellow petals and accented by the deeper yellow stamens; the olive green foliage is splashed with bronze. Does very well in containers. Spread: 3 to 6 feet (1 to 1.8m).

'Escarboucle'
Brilliant red flowers are centered by gold-tipped red stamens: a real knockout. Plus, it blooms heavily all summer long. Not happy in Zones 8 to 10. Spread: 6 to 7 feet (1.8 to 2m).

'Comanche'
One of the few "changeable" waterlilies: the splendid blossoms open pale apricot and darken to a coppery orange. The stamens are orange. The leaves also undergo a change, starting out plum purple and ending up dark green. Plant this one near the edge of your pool so you can admire the show. Spread: 6 to 12 feet (1.8 to 3.7m).

'Fabiola' ('Pink Beauty')
A gorgeous pink, with darker outside petals that make each bloom look as though it were the work of a watercolorist. Best of all, the plant pumps them out continuously. Spread: 4 to 7 feet (1.2 to 2m).

'Gladstone' ('Gladstoniana')

This big plant thrives in larger pools, bearing glorious, cup-shaped, pure white flowers accented with golden stamens. Spread: 6 to 12 feet (1.8 to 3.7m).

'Helvola'

'Helvola' ('Yellow Pygmy')

One of the few small-flowered hybrid waterlilies, it bears loads of tiny, 2- to 4-inch (5 to 10cm), full-petaled, star-shaped blooms in a consistent shade of primrose yellow. Ideal for containers. Spread: 3 feet (1m).

'James Brydon'

Considered by many water gardeners to be the best red. The broad-petaled, cup-shaped flowers are crimson with dramatically contrasting deep orange stamens. (In intense summer heat, however, they fade to a pale rose.) The foliage is handsomely marbled. Suitable for containers. Spread: 5 to 6 feet (1.5 to 1.8m).

'Joey Tomocik'

This sunny yellow charmer has the added plus of spicy fragrance. The flowers tend to rise above the water surface a few inches (7cm or so), like those of a tropical. The foliage is a neat apple green mottled with maroon markings. Spread: 5 feet (1.5m) or more.

'Lucida'

'Lucida'

An elegant plant with star-shaped, pale-rose-pink flowers, set against marbled leaves. Not a large plant, and thus well suited to containers. Spread: 3 to 7 feet (1 to 2m).

'Marliac White' ('Marliac Albida')

3- to 7-inch (7.5 to 18cm) flowers of ice-cream white, punctuated at the center by butterscotch yellow stamens, are produced in abundance on a vigorous plant. The leaves are a deep green. Spread: 6 to 12 feet (1.8 to 3.7m).

'Paul Hariot'

Another changeable, compact enough for growing in containers. The fascinating flowers open a warm yellow, mature to a dark peachy pink, and in cooler climates, finish scarlet. The foliage is mottled with crimson, making a spectacular contrast, especially to the last-day blooms. Spread: 4 to 6 feet (1.2 to 1.8m).

'Perry's Fire Opal'

One of many excellent hybrid waterlilies from Perry Slocum, this one is aptly named. The double, star-shaped flowers are a fabulous, vibrant pink, well complemented by the bronze-hued leaves. Spread: 6 feet (1.8m).

'Pink Sensation'

A dependable pink lily, it has the added bonus of staying open later in the day than some of its fellows. Also, it holds its flowers above the water surface like a tropical. A pretty choice for containers. Spread: 4 to 5 feet (1.2 to 1.5m).

'Sioux'

The changeable blooms of this terrific lily slowly open yellow and become tangerine red. Dark olive-green leaves with maroon splashes make a perfect foil. Can be grown in containers. Spread: 4 to 5 feet (1.2 to 1.5m).

'Texas Dawn'

'Texas Dawn'

A big, vigorous plant with many sterling qualities. The generous, golden yellow blossoms are star-shaped, semidouble, and up to 8 inches (20cm) across, and are held above the water surface like a tropical. They emit a sweet, seductive fragrance.

Best of all, they are produced in profusion—some water gardeners report that 'Texas Dawn' produces more blooms per plant than any other hardy! Spread: 6 to 12 feet (1.8 to 3.7m).

'Virginalis'

This spectacular lily's flowers are cup-shaped and may reach 12 inches (30cm) across, extraordinary for a hardy. Not a pure white, the outer petals have a slight pink tinge; the stamens are bright yellow. It may take a season or two to hit its stride. Spread: 6 to 12 feet (1.8 to 3.7m).

'Albert Greenberg'

TROPICAL WATERLILIES
'Albert Greenberg'

A sweetly fragrant lily with very pretty flowers—warm yellow suffused with a candied, rosy pink, with bright yellow stamens at the center. It blooms earlier and continues longer into autumn than most tropicals. The mint-green leaves are splashed with purple. Does well in containers. Spread: 6 to 7 feet (1.8 to 2m).

'Baghdad'

'Baghdad'

This is a dramatic lily, sporting full, flat, periwinkle-blue flowers with rich yellow stamens. The apple green leaves are splashed with maroon markings and are slightly viviparous. Spread: 7 feet (2m).

'Dauben' ('Daubeniana')

Loads of lovely, miniature (2- to 4-inch [5 to 10cm]) light blue flowers and an easygoing nature make this lily a perfect choice for a beginner's first pool or tub garden. It tolerates shade and withstands cold temperatures better than most. Very viviparous. Spread: 3 to 4 feet (1 to 1.2m).

'Director George T. Moore'

The dark violet petals of this popular lily encircle a golden center; the green leaves are flecked with violet—a fabulous, dramatic sight, sure to take your breath away. Spread: 6 to 7 feet (1.8 to 2m).

'General Pershing'

This is the most famous, most popular pink tropical. Intensely fragrant, the large flowers have a double complement of orchid pink petals and lemon yellow stamens. They stay open all day, several hours longer than most, and are held closer to the water's surface than most tropicals. The rich green leaves are splashed with royal purple. A robust, regal plant. Spread: 6 to 12 feet (1.8 to 3.7m).

'Green Smoke'

Despite its exotic appearance, this lily is not difficult to grow. The aqua-green petals blend with light blue toward the tips, hence the name. Its bronze-green leaves are lightly speckled. Spread: 6 to 12 feet (1.8 to 3.7m).

'Marian Strawn'

Rich fragrance and double white flowers make this lily a showpiece. The forest green leaves are large and sport dark green flecks. Spread: 6 to 12 feet (1.8 to 3.7m).

'Mrs. George H. Pring'

Another white day-bloomer, this one needs lots of space. Its fragrant flowers are massive, up to 13 inches (33cm) across, and a soft white, almost to the point of being translucent. Spread: 9 to 12 feet (2.7 to 3.7m).

'Mrs. Martin E. Randig'

An utterly luscious flower: dark purple petals, dark rose-pink sepals, and a radiant golden center. It's also one of the most deliciously fragrant lilies around. The leaves are a bronzy green and highly viviparous. Spread: 4 to 5 feet (1.2 to 1.5m).

Nymphaea colorata

This is an African species with lovely lilac flowers and dark stamens, set against matte green leaves. A good candidate for a container garden. Spread: 3 to 6 feet (1 to 1.8m).

Nymphaea gigantea

Also known as the Australian waterlily, its sky blue blossoms are held high above the water's surface, even to the point of drooping back downward. And they last as long as a week. It isn't always gigantic; size depends on the strain you grow. Color on some may be nearly white. Spread: varies.

'Panama Pacific'

This stunning vivid purple lily has purple-tipped yellow stamens, and blooms prolifically. The foliage is rather bronzy, with speckles, and is viviparous. It will adjust to small pools, yet expand eagerly in big ones. Spread: 3 to 12 feet (1 to 3.7m).

'Shirley Bryne'

A deep raspberry-sherbet pink flower with sparkling gold stamens within adds up to a uniquely beautiful display. This lily is also quite viviparous, unusual for a pink. It tolerates partial shade. Spread: 5 to 6 feet (1.5 to 1.8m).

'St. Louis Gold'

This buttery yellow lily is an enthusiastic bloomer. Its habit is compact enough for smaller pools and containers. Spread: 6 to 7 feet (1.8 to 2m).

'Yellow Dazzler'

Double, gleaming yellow blooms are produced in abundance and stay open until dusk. The petals of mature flowers splay outward and exude a heady fragrance. The dark green foliage is speckled with bronze. Spread: 6 to 10 feet (1.8 to 3m).

NIGHT-BLOOMING TROPICALS

'Antares'

A classy, breathtaking plant with wine-red flowers displayed against bronze foliage. This one positively thrives in heat and humidity. Spread: 6 feet (1.8m).

'Emily Grant Hutchings'

The full-petaled blooms are deep rose with a hint of magenta; the foliage is bronze. Spread: 6 to 12 feet (1.8 to 2.7m).

'H.C. Haarstick'

A large plant with large flowers, this waterlily has rich, silky red petals and magenta tipped stamens, all set on a field of bronze leaves. Spread: 6 to 12 feet (1.8 to 3.7m).

'Missouri'

Classic, heavy-textured white petals soar above dark green foliage that is bronze when young. On a summer evening, the blooms virtually glow in the dark. Spread: 6 to 12 feet (1.8 to 3.7m).

'Mrs. George C. Hitchcock'

This old favorite is treasured for its robust, flawless blooms with somewhat narrow petals of rose pink; the foliage is maroon flecked with dark green. Spread: 6 to 12 feet (1.8 to 3.7m).

'Red Flare'

'Red Flare'

A superb elaboration on a theme: starry garnet flowers are held high on maroon stems, against a backdrop of maroon-tinted foliage. Plus, it's fragrant—some liken the scent to camphor. Spread: 6 to 7 feet (1.8 to 2m).

'Wood's White Knight'

Considered by many to be the classic white night-bloomer. Luminous, fragrant, star-shaped, semidouble blooms of pure white are centered by cognac-gold stamens. The leaves are emerald green. Spread: 6 to 12 feet (1.8 to 3.7m).

LOTUS

There are few sights as magnificent as a lotus in a water garden, its fabulous, deliciously fragrant, cup-shaped blossoms fully unfurled and dramatic foliage soaring into the air. The flowers come in soft shades of pink, white, yellow, and rose, and after they pass, which is generally three days for individual blossoms, the amazing seedpod is revealed. The tall-stalked leaves (up to 7 feet [2m] tall!) are also extraordinary in their own right for their handsome texture and the way their surface sheds water like quicksilver droplets—children love to lean over a pool's edge and repeatedly splash water on them.

Lotuses are not as frail as you might think, nor are they any harder to grow than many other water garden plants. And although they look almost tropical, they're actually as winter-hardy as any hardy waterlily. A happy lotus plant can even become a pest in the pool, enthusiastically pumping out plenty of foliage and sending chains of tubers growing beyond the bounds of its pot. Water gardeners who have small pools should avoid lotus. Set your sights on no more than one scene-stealing specimen, and be prepared to give up space you might have devoted to other large plants, especially waterlilies. You might try growing a dwarf variety, of which there are a few. The dwarfs can be grown in large tubs, too. And—beginning water garden-ers take note, for this is something the catalogs do not trumpet—often a lotus plant will not bloom its first year. This means you will have to overwinter it and keep dreaming patiently of those fabulous blossoms. Some water gardeners have achieved first-year blooms when they were able to give the plants an early start indoors and fertilized them frantically (every week or two) throughout the growing season.

You should also know that the time of glory is not long. Most lotuses bloom for two months or less, starting and finishing later the farther north you live. Also, your schedule had better allow you to be home during the daytime, for the blossoms close by midafternoon.

WHAT LOTUSES REQUIRE Like waterlilies, they need to grow in still water. And even more than waterlilies, they must have plenty of sunlight, at least six hours a day. They must also have consistently warm water, 80°F (27°C) or hotter, week in and week out, or they will languish and even die. (But before water gardeners in the Deep South rejoice, note that lotuses dislike close, humid air, which inhibits their flowering.) Standard-size lotus plants require plenty of room: a generous pot, at least 6 inches (15cm) deep and 2 feet (61cm) in diameter, in a large pool is best; they don't like water that is too deep, and are happiest immersed in just 2 inches (5cm). And they're greedy feeders, requiring twice-a-month fertilizing with the same food you use for your waterlilies.

For gardeners who are able to provide the conditions a lotus needs to thrive, the magnificent display is nearly effortless. For the rest, growing this plant well is either a triumph of skill and persistence, or a source of endless frustration.

A NOTE ON LOTUS HARDINESS Though tropical in appearance, the lotus is actually a winter-hardy deciduous plant in Zones 4 to 10, blooming reliably in most regions of North America. In the Deep South and Gulf Coast areas, they may not grow as tall, and this may actually be a blessing. To overwinter a lotus, treat it like a hardy waterlily plant, protecting it from freezing (see instructions for overwintering in Chapter Four, Maintenance).

SELECTIONS You may have seen the native American lotus, *Nelumbo lutea*, growing naturally in ponds. The flowers are smaller than the garden hybrids, at 6 to 10 inches (15 to 25cm) across, and a sunny shade of yellow. The foliage has a hint of blue, reminiscent of some hostas. Some nurseries offer it, and it can certainly prosper in a home water garden, but you may be more tempted by the showier hybrids. Nearly all garden hybrids are descended from the spectacular Asian lotus, *Nelumbo nucifera*, which is somewhat less hardy but contributes the genes for the larger flower size. The flowers are most often single-form, although some boast a double complement of petals for a full, almost peonylike appearance.

'Alba Grandiflora'
This one has enormous white flowers, a flash of golden stamens in the center, and intense fragrance. A real showstopper.

'Ben Gibson'
The unique double-petaled flowers are red brushed with white.

'Carolina Queen'
The flowers are a wonderful shade of lilac-pink. The plant may grow taller than most, up to 6 feet (1.8m) tall.

'Charles Thomas'
A smaller plant, suitable for containers, it bears pretty, single, deep lavender-pink blossoms. This is the nearest yet to a lavender lotus.

'Chawan Basu'
Another bicolor bloom, pink and cream. Of shorter stature, at 3 feet (1m) tall, it is a popular choice for containers.

'Maggie Belle Slocum'

This longtime favorite has rich, almost satiny rose-pink blossoms.

'Maggie Belle Slocum'

'Momo Batan'

If you want to try a double-flowered lotus in a container, this is for you. The flowers are dark pink accented by a yellow center.

'Mrs. Perry D. Slocum'

A changeable lotus, not unlike the changeable waterlilies. The lovely flowers open dark pink and gradually change over several days to a soft yellow.

'Perry's Grand Sunburst'

Soft yellow flowers.

'Roseum Plenum'

Fully double rose-pink blossoms.

'Speciosum'

Flowers in a sweet, sugary pink.

MARGINALS

Any plant that tolerates or thrives in shallow water is considered a marginal and suitable for growing in a home water garden. Those of shorter stature are good additions to container gardens. You'll notice that a number of marginals are attractive species plants, unimproved by plant hybridizers. Others have been selected for larger or more profuse flowers, more handsome foliage, and other improvements. The following is a sampling of commonly available marginals. You'll want to watch the catalogs and garden centers for new plants; as the popularity of water gardening grows, the choices are sure to expand.

Many marginals are enthusiastic growers, and are best confined to a pot; as a dividend, this makes tinkering with the design of your display easier. Unless otherwise noted, most will thrive immersed in an inch (2.5cm) of water on a side shelf or elevated support; experiment to find out what suits each one best. To get optimum flowering and assure healthy foliage, fertilize marginals regularly.

SOME NOTES ON DESIGN Marginals provide vertical interest in contrast to the more prostrate waterlilies you may have planted. They can serve as a transition between the outer edges of the pool and the interior, and between the water surface and the surrounding landscape of your garden.

Avoid choosing many plants of similar foliage, something that may not be obvious to you when the plants are in bloom, but that can make for a monotonous display after the flowers pass.

A NOTE ON HARDINESS Some marginals are winter-hardy in cold climates (generally speaking, in Plant Hardiness Zones 4 to 10), while others are tropicals that must be rescued and overwintered indoors at season's end, or discarded in favor of a fresh start next year. They are so identified at the end of each description below. See the previous chapter for overwintering information.

SELECTIONS

Acorus calamus, sweet flag

Sweet flag has slender, lance-shaped leaves that grow to between 2 and 4 feet (61 to 122cm). The common name comes from the fact that, when crushed, the leaves emit a pleasant, citrusy fragrance. In spring it flowers with tiny green blossoms, but the plant is mainly valued as an always-handsome foliage accent plant. Also available is 'Variegatus', which has white-to-cream stripes. Hardy.

Acorus gramineus, Japanese or dwarf sweet flag

A more slender, shorter plant than its cousin, between 8 and 18 inches (20 to 46cm) tall. Grow this one in just an inch (2.5cm) or so of water. It does well in container water gardens. 'Variegatus' sports yellow stripes. Hardy.

Butomus umbellatus, flowering rush

The slim, sharp-edged green leaves of this rushlike plant grow to between 2 and 3 feet (61 to 100cm) tall, and in mid- through late summer are joined by umbels of rosy pink flowers. Makes a pretty partner for the blue-flowered marginal pickerel weed (*Pontederia cordata*), which also blooms later. Can be grown in a larger container garden. Hardy.

Caltha palustris, marsh marigold

The glossy leaves are rounded and waxy, and the masses of buttercuplike flowers appear in loose clusters in spring. The plant may grow up to 2 feet (61cm) high, and spreads outward by means of runners, which you should clip off not only to rein in the plant but also to encourage more flowering. A nice choice for pools that favor bright primary colors. Hardy.

Canna × generalis, canna lily

The aquatic cannas, which may reach a towering 6 feet (1.8m), are spectacular additions to water gardens. They have big, dramatic leaves (sometimes striped), and bear tall stalks of fabulous flowers with large petals in bright shades of red, pink, yellow, and orange. Look for the Longwood hybrids, among them 'Endeavor', which is clear red, 'Erebus', which is pink, 'Ra', which is yellow, and 'Taney', which is salmon orange. All look good with waterlilies of similar hues, particularly the tropicals; they do tend to steal the show from other marginals, however, because of their size. Tropical.

Canna Lily

Carex, sedges

Sedges look like thin grasses at first glance, but they have three-sided blades and are commonly seen in or near ponds in nature. A few are "in cultivation," meaning that you can find them at nurseries that supply water gardeners. Two good choices are Bowles' golden sedge (*Carex elata* 'Bowles' Golden'), which contributes sunny yellow blades that are pretty next to yellow waterlilies and irises, and Japanese sedge *(Carex morrowii)*, whose blue-green foliage is a handsome counterpart to hardy waterlily foliage and blooms. Hardy.

Colocasia, taro

Some of the most spectacular foliage plants you can add to a water garden display, taros have big, velvety leaves that reach 3 or more feet (1m or more). These shed water the way lotus leaves do, and may be marked with purple or cranberry red, or have contrasting

Colocasia esculenta

margins or veins. They grow from a tuber; plant several inches (10cm or so) deep in an ample pot, making sure not to cover the growing tip. Cultivars include 'Illustris' (leaves feature black markings), 'Euchlora' (dark leaves with royal purple margins), and 'Fontanesii' (violet stems). Tropical.

Cyperus alternifolius, umbrella palm

This easy-to-grow classic for garden pools tops out between 1 and 2 feet (30 to 61cm). It has grassy leaves that are bright green; the flowers themselves grow in brown umbels. Can be submerged up to 6 inches (15cm). Use at one end of the pool as an accent, or elevate several in the center for a dramatic, tropical-looking focal point. *Cyperus papyrus*, the Egyptian papyrus, grows 4 to 10 feet (1.2 to 3m). Tropical.

Cyperus haspan, dwarf papyrus

A smaller, more delicate *Cyperus* species, with fuller, tufted flower heads. Stays under 2 feet (61cm) tall. It does very well in containers. Tropical.

Eleocharis montevidensis, spike rush

This is a perky little clump-forming accent plant for the pool edge or a container garden, growing no more than a foot (30cm) high. It sports slender but straight leaves that are tipped with tiny brown "flower" nubs. Place in just an inch or two (2.5 to 5cm) of water. Hardy.

Equisetum hyemale, horsetail

Tall and upright, this plant is neither a grass nor a rush, but rather their simple, hollow-tubed ancestor. Its appeal lies in the way its bright green stalks are divided by black joints. Several pots of horsetail will form a solid, 4- to 5-foot (1.2 to 1.5cm) screen at the back of the pool. Submerge them in no more than 4 inches (10cm) of water. Owners of small pools beware: this handsome plant is an enthusiastic grower and tends to exceed its bounds quickly. Hardy.

Glyceria maxima 'Variegata', manna grass

A white-striped clump-forming grass that does well in water gardens. It reaches 2 feet (61cm) tall at most, but its bright demeanor calls attention to it wherever it is placed in the pool. Doesn't do well in Zones 9 and 10. Hardy.

Houttuynia cordata 'Variegata'

Grown for its low mats of gorgeous variegated foliage, this wandering perennial plant can become a pest in damp spots in the garden proper, but is a wonderful potted addition to a pool. The 3-inch (7.5cm), heart-shaped leaves are randomly splashed with rosy pink and creamy white; if they appear, the flowers are small white spikes that don't last long. Wonderful near the surface-floating blooms of a pink or white hardy waterlily, in the pool or in a container garden. Set the pots in an inch (2.5cm) or so of water, and keep after the plants, pruning if they grow too vigorously. Hardy.

Houttuynia cordata

Hydrocleys nymphoides, water poppy

A bold plant both in appearance and in its growing habits, and so best used in larger pools. The bright yellow, 2-inch (5cm), 3-petaled flowers look a bit like poppies and are produced in profu-sion above a mass of shiny, oval leaves. Splendid in the company of yellow waterlilies. Tropical.

Iris ensata or *I. kaempferi*, Japanese iris

One of the many irises that enjoys life in a water garden. There are numerous selections, mainly in crisp shades of white or purple. Grows between 2 and 3 feet (61cm to 1m) tall, so it flatters waterlilies and many other marginals rather than overwhelming them. A clump of white-flowered Japanese iris is stunning in front of any of the white tropical waterlilies. Hardy.

Iris pseudacorus, yellow flag

A reliable bloomer for the edge of the pool is the cheery yellow flag. It reaches heights of 3 feet (1m), and spreads modestly over the years. It can grow in moist soil or in up to a foot (30cm) of water, and looks particularly nice when massed. One with white-striped leaves, 'Variegata', is available. Hardy.

Iris sibirica, Siberian iris

These lovely irises come in shades of blue, lavender, purple, white, and even yellow. They grow as easily as the others, and attain 3 feet (1m) in height. Hardy.

Iris versicolor, blue flag

A tough but pretty plant with flowers of blue or purple; grows 3 feet (1m) tall. Hardy.

Lobelia cardinalis, cardinal flower

A wildflower sometimes seen along streams and in damp places in nature, cardinal flower adapts easily to the water garden. Clumps generally sport several stems, each topped with a bright crimson flower. Some nurseries offer cultivated varieties in shades of magenta, pink, or white. At 18 or more inches (46cm or more) tall, it can become a little gangly for smaller pools. Makes a splendid companion for white irises or blue pickerel rush. Hardy.

Mentha, mint

If you want an attractive foliage plant that spreads outward rather than upward, with the added bonus of sweet fragrance (noticeable when you bruise the foliage with your fingers), try adding mint to your water garden. *Mentha aquatica*, with its fuzzy, rounded leaves, is a natural choice, but you might experiment with growing its relatives. *Mentha citrata* has leaves with a bronzy cast and a nicer fragrance. All mints adore water. Confined to a pot, your water garden inhabitant may still need to be restrained by occasional trimming. Hardy.

Menyanthes trifolata, bog bean

Relatively low-growing (a foot [30cm] high at most), the dependable little plant known as bog bean is ideal for filling in open spots on the pool surface or softening the edges. The lobed, dark green leaves look a bit like broad bean foliage, hence the name. They are joined in late spring by small spikes of lacy-petaled flowers that begin as rosy pink buds but open a creamy white. Hardy.

Nymphoides, water snowflake

The name water snowflake applies to several fast-growing, spreading plants with small, lacy flowers. Their leaves, up to 6 inches (15cm) across, are roundish or heart-shaped, and float on the water surface. They are usually emerald green, though you may find some with variegated leaves. *N. cristata* and *N. indica* have white flowers; *N. crenata* has yellow flowers. Because water snowflakes are somewhat reminiscent of little waterlilies, they're useful for providing coverage of the water surface of a pool or as a small, pretty substitute for waterlilies in container gardens. Tropical.

Nymphoides peltata, floating heart

Closely related to water snowflake, and used in the same ways, floating heart looks even more like a mini-waterlily. The floating leaves, about 3 inches (7.5cm) in diameter, are splashed with maroon markings, and the sunny yellow flowers (not fringed) are held slightly above the water surface. Tropical.

Orontium aquaticum

Orontium aquaticum, golden club

The foliage—stalks of oval, dark green leaves up to a foot (30cm) long—is good-looking, but not especially exciting. The flowers, on the other hand, are intriguing, and make quite a show in spring and early summer. They're actually thin white spikes tipped with gold, and reach about 4 inches (10cm) high. This plant is a welcome addition to pools where early color is desired, before the waterlilies and other aquatics really hit their stride. Hardy.

Peltandra virginica, arrow arum

Grown mainly for its textured foliage, arrow arum forms clumps of deeply veined, arrow-shaped leaves about a foot (30cm) long, on 2- to 3-foot (61cm to 1m) stalks. The flowers, borne on a small spathe, are green, and are followed later in the season by bronze-green berries. Arrow arum is a good choice where you want a bold display. Hardy.

Phalaris arundinacea 'Picta', variegated gardener's garters

Although technically a grass, gardener's garters looks more like a bamboo, making it a natural for Japanese-style water gardens or those where a screen of foliage is wanted. This popular variety is striped white and reaches 2 to 3 feet (60 to 90cm). Hardy.

Pontederia cordata, pickerel rush or pickerel weed

A handsome, easygoing plant, this clump-former has spear shaped leaves up to 3 feet (1m) long. They are joined in midsummer by wonderful blue to purple flower spikes that continue blooming until early autumn. Splendid in combination with the yellow or pink flowers of many waterlilies and marginals, but not as satisfactory with blue flowers because the color is hard to match. It is also available in a white version, and a pink one has appeared in the mail-order catalogs in recent years. Hardy.

Sagittaria, arrowhead

Long a favorite of water gardeners, arrowhead has plenty to recommend it: The broad, arrow-shaped leaves are dramatic, and the 3-petaled flowers, carried in clusters atop tall stems, are gorgeous. *S. latifolia*, which grows to only 2 feet (61cm) tall, has white flowers with a splash of yellow in the center. It is a nice addition to a container garden. *S. montevidensis*, about twice as tall, has more exotic-looking flowers—the petals are still white, but the base of each one has a wine-red mark. You may also find the *S. sagittifolia* cultivar 'Flore Pleno', about 2 feet (61cm) tall, which has so many petals the flowers are downright fluffy, almost like small white carnations. The taller ones are well suited to any size pool, and look great in and out of flower. Hardy.

Saururus cernuus, lizard's tail

A short accent plant best suited to the edges of a pool or container water gardens, lizard's tail forms clumps of apple green, heart-shaped leaves about 2 feet (61cm) tall. Its slender, nodding spikes of creamy white flowers exude a faintly sweet, citrusy fragrance. They are followed by slightly puckered greenish fruits that may have inspired the common name. Hardy.

Thalia dealbata, hardy water canna

Similar to its tropical cousins, hardy water canna has graceful oblong leaves; the flowers are carried on stalks and are light blue to purple. It grows to between 2 and 6 feet (61cm to 1.8m) tall. A fine choice for water gardens whose design would benefit from such a tall plant. Looks great in combination with tall cyperus. Hardy only to Zone 6.

Typha, cattail

No water garden would be complete without some cattails, and there are a number of attractive, manageable-size ones in cultivation. Their distinctive brown catkin "flowers" appear in late summer, but the foliage is a graceful contribution all season long. The tallest cattail for water gardens is probably *T. latifolia*, at a towering 7 to 9 feet (2 to 2.7m). The shortest one, short enough even for inclusion in container gardens, is the grassy-leaved, 2-foot (61cm) *T. minima*. A cultivar of this called 'Europa' is even smaller, at 1 to 2 feet (30 to 60cm) high. There are several in-between options, including *T. laxmannii*, the aptly named graceful cattail. Hardy.

FLOATERS

Plants that float on the water's surface are important elements in a water garden. They tend to have handsome foliage, and a few flower. Usually you do not pot them, but rather, just toss them into the water. Along with the lilypads, their purpose is to contribute to the desirable two-thirds surface coverage. Floaters will thrive so long as the water is not too sterile, as their roots derive nourishment directly from the water. Algae also likes waterborne nutrients, so adding floaters can help solve your algae problem. Also, their trailing roots offer fish a place to hide or spawn.

Be forewarned that floaters reproduce themselves quickly, either by offsets or division. You may start off with what you fear is too few, and soon find you have too many. Ruthlessly thin out unwanted growth or completely remove excess plants. Discard them on the compost pile, never down the storm drain or any other place where they might make their way into local waterways and become a pest.

A NOTE ON HARDINESS Most floating plants are tropical and thrive when the pool's water is warm. They should be removed prior to the first frost. You can treat them as annuals, tossing them on the compost pile at season's end and buying new plants the following year.

SELECTIONS
Azolla caroliniana and *A. filiculoides*, fairy moss or water fern
Not technically a fern, the rampant-growing fairy moss forms mats of 2-lobed leaves on short stems. As they age, the leaves gain a reddish tint. Tropical.

Eichhornia crassipes, water hyacinth
Water hyacinth is both a beauty and a beast. It has glossy green leaves and spikes of lovely purple or lavender (occasionally white) flowers. The spongy stems are inflated, and the feathery roots trail below, enabling the plant to float. In nature, however, it has become a terrible pest, and has clogged rivers and lakes in the South, where it has been banned from commerce. Tropical.

Lemna minor, duckweed
No one ever really buys the dainty-looking duckweed—it generally hitches a ride in on the roots or foliage of new waterlilies and marginals. It's tiny, no more than a half-inch (12mm) across, com-

posed of 2 to 4 (usually 3) leaves. Duckweed reproduces quickly, floats freely, and is moved about by wind. Your fish may dine on it, as may visiting birds, but if you find your pool overwhelmed, it's not difficult to sift out excess. Complete eradication, on the other hand, is practically impossible. Hardy.

Eichhornia crassipes

Limnobium spongia, frog's bit
The lusty growing frog's bit has small apple-green basal leaves, about a half-inch (1.5cm) across or less, with spongy undersides that enable it to float. It reproduces by offsets. Tropical.

Ludwigia sedidiodes
A relatively new plant to cultivation, this gorgeous but delicate floater forms an ever-expanding mat of small green leaves in diamondlike shapes; the effect is as though someone had spilled a bowl of green gems. Pot it in soil and immerse it in about 4 inches (10cm) of water. Tropical.

Marsilea mutica, water clover
Each cloverlike plant is 3 inches (7.5cm) across, in shades of green with accents of white, yellow, or bronze; because it's a fern relative, there are no flowers. It forms small matlike colonies. Pot in soil and immerse in 6 inches (15cm) of water. Hardy.

Neptunia oleracea, neptunia

Neptuna is a lot of fun because it's sensitive. The stems are lined with tiny, red-rimmed leaves that fold inward when touched. It grows relatively slowly and stays afloat by means of spongy white tissue attached to the stems. It will root in soil. Tropical.

Pistia stratiotes, water lettuce

The handsome, 6-inch (15cm) water lettuce leaves invite touching—they are soft and velvety and, like lotuses and taro, shed droplets of water when splashed. Water lettuce is sensitive to sun (too much causes the leaves to turn yellow), so it is best used in pools or containers that don't receive all-day sun. Note that it has been banned in Texas and some other southern states. Tropical.

Salvinia, water fern

The light green leaves of the water fern, under an inch (2.5cm), are furry with tiny hairs. The plant forms extended chains or mats and often needs thinning. Try it alone in a small, attractive container garden for a real conversation piece. Tropical.

Wolffia, water meal

Even smaller than the similar duckweed, water meal leaves are no more than 1/16 inch (1.5mm) in diameter, and bright green. It forms large, free-floating colonies. Tropical.

OXYGENATING PLANTS

You plant these not for their good looks, though some are attractive, but for the vital part they play in keeping your water garden healthy. They keep down the algae population by starving it out, contribute oxygen to the pool environment, and nourish the fish as well. If you peer down into the water at them, or haul out strands while thinning, you may actually see tiny bubbles percolating from their foliage into the surrounding water.

These plants should always be grown in pots, which anchor them and may help control their growth. They can be submerged deep in the middle of the pool, or in the shallow areas on the edge. Do allow them to become established before adding fish, however, because fish may nudge or nibble them right out of their pots before they are fully rooted. When pruning, don't yank—use clippers or scissors.

A NOTE ON HARDINESS Tropical or hardy, cultivated oxygenating plants are so inexpensive and prolific, there's really no point in trying to overwinter them. If you wish to, though, it's simply a matter of removing them from the pool during the end-of-season cleanup, and keeping them indoors in an aquarium.

SELECTIONS

Cabomba, fanwort

The stems of fanwort display lacy, fan-shaped leaves in hues anywhere from bright green to a reddish brown. Hardy to Zone 6.

Elodea canadensis, anacharis or waterweed

The branched stems of anacharis are laden with clusters of bright green whorled leaves. Hardy.

Myriophyllum aquaticum, parrot's feather

Probably the best-looking of the lot, and a plant that does not remain demurely underwater, parrot's feather likes to pokes gracefully above and trail along the water's surface. The bright green, unbranched stems are lined with feathery whorls of leaves. Hardy.

Sagittaria natans, Old-World arrowhead

Ribbony leaves of dark green. Hardy.

Vallisneria americana, ribbon grass

Almost translucent, ribbonlike leaves. Fares well in deeper pools. Hardy.

APPENDICES
EQUIPMENT OPTIONS

The addition of special electrical appliances to your water garden, if it's a small one, is nearly always optional. Even so, a pump or filter can benefit the life in your pool (especially in the case of fish) and reduce maintenance, while a fountain, waterfall, or lights will enhance its appearance and your enjoyment of it.

GENERAL SAFETY As everyone knows, mixing water and electricity can be a risky business. If you are not confident of your ability to install a device, get experienced help. A licensed electrician can certainly handle any routine installation.

No matter who performs the installation, you can rest easy knowing that all appliances intended for use in a water garden are designed with the proper insulation and safety features. Just make sure that all electrical connections are heavy-duty, weatherproof ones intended for outdoor use, and that the outlet is grounded (that it can accept a three-prong plug). Whatever the equipment you install, invest in a "ground fault current interrupter" (GFCI). This is an extension cord–style accessory that shuts off power when it detects a leak in the electrical current, thus preventing shock. Some have a reset feature that automatically engages after danger is past, a feature you may find valuable.

PUMPS The main purpose of a pump in a water garden is to keep the water circulating. A pump is a good idea for pools larger than 800 gallons (2.4 kl), to keep the oxygen moving. You'll also need one if you plan to install a filter, fountain, or waterfall. And should you ever need to empty your pool, a pump will make that job much easier.

Water-garden pump technology has come a long way. You can find a quiet, compact, submersible pump for a reasonable price. Traditionally pumps have been energy hogs, but more efficient models are now available. Shop around, and ask the vendor lots of questions to make sure you are buying a pump that is appropriate for your needs.

The first thing you should know when shopping for a pump is your pool's capacity in gallons (kl), because pumps are rated as to their output in gallons (kl) per hour (see page 47 for the formula that will help you calculate this number). Ideally, a pump should "turn over" the entire pool in an hour. It's wise to pick out a pump capable of 25 to 50 percent more, just so it is not working full time at its maximum capacity, and to allow you some flexibility; for instance, if you don't always clean the filter in a timely manner, at least the pump will still meet the pool's needs. If you plan to install a waterfall, the pump will have to work harder, so you'll definitely want to invest in a more powerful model.

To get the best performance from your pump, don't set it on the pool bottom, where it may become clogged with silt. Instead, place it on a shelf or otherwise elevate it. Set it up away from waterlilies and other plants that dislike turbulence.

You may leave your pump in the water all winter, provided it remains immersed and your pool doesn't freeze solid. Run it occasionally to circulate toxic gases that may build up in the deep water and release them out into the air. By moving the water every now and then, a pump can also help keep the pool "open," that is, prevent it from freezing over.

FILTERS Although oxygenating plants go a long way toward helping to keep your pool water clear, you may still wish to install a filter with your pump. Filters make pool maintenance easier by removing suspended organic particles from the water. They are especially useful when you have a lot of fish fouling the water, or if your pool tends to heat up due to its small size or location in full sun, accelerating the decay of organic matter.

As when shopping for other pool equipment, ask the vendor questions to determine you are getting exactly what you want. The vendor should also provide information on installation and maintenance. Be sure to buy some extra pads to have on hand when it's time for replacements. Following is an overview of the various choices.

micron: A very fine filter that controls algae, making it ideal for pools that are more landscape ornaments than gardens—that is, pools that don't have natural help in remaining clear, and that don't have fish.

sand: Best for larger pools, especially ones with more fish and fewer plants. Sand catches fish waste and heavier particles, converting it to backwash that you can use elsewhere in your garden.

biological: This is a heavy-duty filter, generally situated outside the pool in a weatherproof housing. It does need a pump to deliver water to it and return the cleaned water back to the pool. A biological filter effectively removes all sorts of debris, plus it provides a stable environment for "good" bacteria that convert harmful fish waste into helpful plant fertilizer. The best biofilters are designed to add oxygen to the system.

FOUNTAINS AND WATERFALLS In addition to the obvious benefits of pleasant sights and sounds, fountains and waterfalls can be practical additions. They recirculate the water and help keep the pool environment aerated. Of course, they require a pump to run them. When shopping for a fountain or waterfall, take a look at kits, which save you the trouble of wondering whether all your equipment is compatible.

Before you leap, consider where in your water garden the fountain or waterfall will go. Remember that waterlilies need still water, and position the action as far from them as possible. A vigorous fountain or waterfall may also rattle or even tumble nearby potted plants. Fountains are available in great variety, from little bubbles to dramatically tiered affairs. Waterfalls can be homemade, if you prefer that to the store-bought kits. Again, shop around, and get expert advice before making a final decision.

LIGHTING Well-chosen and properly installed lighting can bring a whole new dimension to your enjoyment of your pool. Some water gardeners have found that less is better; too many beams bouncing off the variety of plants creates glare and confusing shadows rather than the hoped-for drama. Adjustable lights, whether installed on nearby trees or closer to the ground, will allow you to tinker until you are satisfied with the result. If you want to install low-voltage lighting right in the pool, consult a qualified electrician early in your planning process. Bear in mind that this is most effective in pools that are well filtered and fairly clear.

FISH MATTERS

There are many good reasons to add fish to your water garden. They're beautiful and fun to watch, adding to the pleasure of having a pool. They're practical to have around, too; fish are an important ingredient in the pool's ecological balance. They dine on mosquito larvae and other insects, nibble algae off plants, and even eat decaying material. And the carbon dioxide that is a by-product of their respiration is immediately available to your plants.

WHAT KIND? There is a wide range of choices, from the cheapest goldfish to very expensive koi. Shop at a local pet store or garden center, or look over the interesting selection in some mail-order water-garden catalogs. Mail-order fish are shipped overnight or by second-day air in plastic bags of water, with care instructions. Whatever your source for fish, seek out fish with colorful markings because they show up best in dark water. Patterned ones, and even all-white ones, are easiest to see.

A word of caution about koi: they are expensive, and they have special needs. Due to their size, they require a larger, deeper pool. In a pool too small for them, they are like bulls in a china shop, knocking over or dislodging plants, and stirring sediment up from the bottom to the upper, warmer layers, making the water murky and providing ideal conditions for algae to thrive. They're also hearty eaters—you cannot expect them to get by on mosquito larvae. They'll dine eagerly and often on anything from special fish food pellets, to common earthworms, to your plants. Koi have sensitive systems compared to those of ordinary goldfish, so you may find it necessary to invest in a filter. So, with all these disadvantages, why would you want koi? Well, they're gorgeous, and they make friendly pets. When they are comfortable, they may even greet you at the pool's edge in hope of a snack and to be petted.

HOW MANY? Don't overdo. Too many fish can spoil your pool's water quality. The maximum should be one fish per 5 gallons (20 liters) of water, though over time your own experience may counsel a few more or less. Don't forget that the fish will grow and place an increasing burden on the pool environment and filtering system. You can also expect your fish to multiply. If you don't allow for this, you'll have to net the extras and find new homes for them.

INTRODUCING FISH TO THEIR NEW HOME Never add fish to a newly filled pool. You must wait. Allow the chlorine to evaporate or treat the pool to remove chlorine or chloramine, and then let the plants become established. If your pool experiences a severe algal bloom, you must hold off, because the fish cannot survive in such an oxygen-poor setting.

Some experts suggest that new fish be quarantined in a fishbowl or aquarium for several weeks before they are introduced to the pool. This way, you can be sure they are healthy and won't be bringing with them any of the contagious diseases to which domestic fish are susceptible. However, this step shouldn't be necessary if you purchase your fish from a reputable supplier.

Never toss fish into the pool—at the very least, the temperature change may be a shock. Instead, float them on the surface in a water-filled plastic bag for an hour or so, out of direct sunlight, then release them to their new home.

FEEDING YOUR FISH With the exception of koi, the truth is that you don't really have to feed a small population of fish. They'll get by just fine on mosquito larvae, duckweed, and other naturally available food. However, all fish will grow larger and healthier, and be more inclined to reproduce, if you supplement their diet.

Feed small fish on flakes, and larger fish on pellets (if in doubt, get instructions from wherever you bought the fish). How much? That will depend on the type of fish and how active they are. The rule of thumb is to give them only what they will consume in five minutes. Uneaten food will foul the water.

Koi can be real gourmets. In addition to pellets, you can tempt them with worms and grubs as well as food from your own kitchen. They've been known to gobble everything from bread to wheat germ or oatmeal flakes to chopped corn kernels.

BREEDING/SPAWNING Your fish may reproduce without any help from you. As mentioned previously, though, extra food early in the season will encourage them—especially the females. If you look closely, you'll be able to tell which fish are female because they will become noticeably fatter. They lay their eggs in the trailing roots of floating plants, and you will notice them inspecting potential egg-laying sites in advance. Meanwhile, the behavior of the males will give them away. They'll nudge and chase the females around the pool, sometimes so enthusiastically that you'll see them arching out of the water. When the female is ready, she'll release her eggs at her chosen spot and the male, right behind her, will unleash milt to fertilize them. The fry generally hatch in three to seven days.

FRY Baby fish can look quite different from their parents. You might even mistake them for mosquito larvae wiggling around, but they'll grow quickly, especially if you toss in a little flake food for them. As with all little creatures in nature, the road to adulthood is not easy for fry. They are easy targets for visiting birds. They may even be eaten by adult fish! Good plant cover in your pool will give them a fighting chance, but if you are concerned about their survival, catch them with a net and raise them elsewhere.

WINTER CARE So long as your pool does not freeze solid, you can leave your fish outdoors all winter. As the weather grows colder, they'll become less active and eventually retreat to the muck in the bottom, where they'll go into a hibernationlike state. There are steps you can take to help assure their survival. In late summer and autumn, before the water starts to cool, feed them regularly so they head into their winter sleep with reserves of fat. If you've been giving them high-protein foods, switch to high-carbohydrate foods. The goal is to help them build up fat reserves, not induce growth. Once the water temperatures drop into the low 50's and 40's F (about 10°C), stop feeding altogether.

Over the course of the winter, keep after your pool's ice layer. Don't allow the surface to freeze solid, or toxic gases may get trapped and kill the fish. Maintain an opening as described on page 90, so the water remains oxygenated. If you poke through the ice with a branch or stick, avoid stirring up the bottom of the pool; if you disturb the fish, they'll expend valuable energy.

EARLY SPRING CARE On one of your early visits out to the pool after a long winter, you may notice that the fish are in motion again. You may be tempted to feed them as soon as you see them. Don't. Wait until the water temperature rises over 50°F (10°C); the water will warm up more slowly than the air. If you feed your fish too early, and then the temperatures take a dip, your fish won't be able to finish digesting, which is harmful. A stressed fish is more vulnerable to disease. As the water temperature rises, reintroduce food gradually. It is always better to underfeed than overfeed at this point.

WHY FISH DIE Assuming the fish arrived at your water garden in good health, the only other explanation for early death is stress. Fish experience stress if you place them in water that is too cold, or water that contains chlorine or chloramine. Both of these conditions are preventable. Exposed to these conditions, fish may languish and die immediately, or the stress to their systems may make them sick and they'll die of one of the many diseases that afflict fish.

The leading cause of death in otherwise perfectly healthy fish is low oxygen levels. You'll see them gasping at the water's surface. If you have been less than observant, you'll step outdoors one morning, too late, and find their little bodies are floating belly up. The biology of a garden pool is such that during the day, when the sun is shining, the plants are producing oxygen and consuming carbon dioxide, and the animals (fish in particular) are producing carbon dioxide and consuming oxygen. This cycle comes to a halt at nightfall. On hot, muggy summer nights, a number of plants, and particularly underwater "oxygenating" plants, will continue to produce carbon dioxide, and your pool's oxygen level will drop precipitously.

Fortunately, the solution to this problem is simple. Agitate the water to release the carbon dioxide and dissolve oxygen into the water. If you have a fountain or waterfall, run it on such nights. Otherwise, churn the water a bit with a hose spray or even a stick before you go to bed. And pray for rain, which eases this problem naturally.

FISH DISEASES AND TREATMENTS Try to catch an afflicted fish and inspect it carefully. Certain fungus organisms cause sores, a cloudy film over the eyes, or rotting tails and fins. Parasites may cover the body—evident as small red or white spots. If you are in doubt about what is ailing your fish, take it to a reputable fish dealer, pet store, or nursery for a prompt diagnosis. All of these maladies, if caught in time, are treatable. Remedies are sold wherever fish are sold, in the form of liquids that you add to the pool water. Always follow label directions exactly.

WATER QUALITY

THE PRESENCE OF ALGAE ISN'T ALWAYS A PROBLEM Nothing worries new pool owners more than the quality of the water, especially when they see algae. Relax. If you've planned and planted carefully, more than likely your pool will be fine. Unlike a backyard swimming pool, a garden pool isn't meant to be crystal clear. A small amount of algae, visible as a slightly green or bronze cast to the water and as a coating that forms on the sides, is both normal and healthy.

New water gardens inevitably experience an algal bloom. This is because there is plenty of light available to encourage its growth, and dissolved minerals in the water to nourish it. Small or shallow pools and container gardens are most vulnerable because they heat up faster. It's easy to panic, and tempting to scoop out the gobs of algae or empty the pool entirely. The best policy, though, is to wait it out. Once the plants get established and start to cover the water surface, and the pool settles into a state of balance, the algae *will* disappear.

COPING WITH AN ALGAE PROBLEM If your pool is not newly installed and appears overwhelmed with a smelly pea soup of algae, you have a problem—and you have options. As mentioned above, repeatedly hauling out the algae with a stick or net, or emptying and refilling the pool, won't necessarily solve anything unless you discover and address what caused the excessive growth in the first place. What causes algae to grow?

HIGH WATER TEMPERATURE Algae thrives in very warm water. Several long, hot sunny days can sometimes start up an algae problem for the first time. Shallow water, along the pool edge, and especially if you have a shelf, is especially prone to overheating.

Solutions:

• Consider adding more plants, especially waterlilies and others that will give the water surface more coverage. Add more floating plants, which will out-compete the algae for minerals dissolved in the water.

• Cool the water by providing extra shade for the pool. Perhaps even a large umbrella in the heat of the day will do the trick. If you have a side shelf, pay particular attention to shading that area.

EXTRA NUTRIENTS If you've been overfertilizing your aquatic plants, perhaps the excess nutrients have been leaching into the water and nourishing the growth of algae. Fertilizer runoff from your lawn or surrounding garden can also encourage algae.

Solutions:

• Cut back on fertilizing, especially in hot weather, and see if that helps.

• If runoff is getting into your pool, take steps to stop it. Bank up the sides around the pool, or make channels that divert the flow of water away from the water garden.

FISH Overfeeding your fish can lead to an algae problem. The food they don't eat will break down in the water, adding to the organic broth.

Solutions:

• Never feed your fish more than they can consume over a five-minute period.

• Feed them even less if algae is a chronic problem.

Fish excrement, and its by-product ammonia, also encourages the growth of algae.

Solutions:

- You don't have to remove all your fish, but you certainly ought to cut back the population to more balanced levels. (See Chapter 3, Stocking and Planting, for the recommended levels.)
- Install a filter that removes fish waste from the water. (See Equipment Options, page 120; the best choice, but also the most costly, is a biological filter.)

IMPROPER pH LEVEL The most common algae seen in home water gardens is green algae, which thrives in more alkaline water. Reddish algae prefers more acidic water. Invest in a simple pH test kit to determine the pool's pH; the best time to check is first thing in the morning. The ideal level is between 6.8 and 7.4.

Solution:

- Buy a liquid pH-adjusting chemical from a water-garden specialist. Follow the directions on the label exactly.

WILL ADDING A FILTER HELP? Yes. A biological filter can remove some or all of the algae's food sources. A less expensive mechanical filter strains algae and other particles before they break down into algae food.

WILL MOVING WATER HELP? No. The addition of a pump, fountain, or waterfall simply aerates the water, bringing in more oxygen. In fact, too much turbulence will stir up mineral-rich sediment from the bottom of the pool, deliver it to the light and warmth of the upper water layers, and thus fuel continuous production of algae.

A CREATURE THAT EATS ALGAE Your fish will eat some algae, but if you want to really target the green stuff, try water fleas (*Daphnia*). Actually crustaceans, these little creatures will consume nothing but algae. You can find them at pet shops that have fish supplies. Warning: if you have fish, these tasty little fellows might not live long enough to do their job.

Snails graze algae from the sides and eat pond detritus before it breaks down into nutrients.

WATER DYES Pools with few plants, and that therefore lack sufficient plant coverage, are vulnerable to algae growth. Water dyes darken the water, depriving algae of the light it needs to grow. They create an inky, mirrorlike surface that fades over time and will require occasional replenishing.

ABOUT CHEMICAL SOLUTIONS TO ALGAE PROBLEMS Chemical treatment should be your last resort, because a water garden is a complex ecosystem, and in your zeal to eradicate algae, you may inadvertently harm other pool residents. Even when a chemical remedy works well, you'll still have to cope with the dead algae, which generate more nutrients as they rot.

If you decide to try a chemical treatment, be sure to select one specifically designed for use in backyard water gardens, and follow the label instructions exactly. Low doses don't work, and high doses are sure to damage other plants and perhaps pool creatures as well. Note that repeated treatments may be necessary.

One "natural" chemical remedy that has received attention in recent years is straw. Its algae-killing properties were discovered by accident when a British farmer noticed that algae disappeared from a pond on his property after some bales fell in the water. Since then, researchers have established that barley straw is the most effective algae killer, and wheat straw runs a close second. Apply twice year, once in autumn and again in spring, before algae growth has a chance to get started. Not much straw is required. About 2 pounds (1kg) bundled, so it will be easy to recover, will treat a 3-foot (1m)-deep pool that measures about 20 feet by 50 feet (6 by 15m).

OTHER WATER-QUALITY PROBLEMS

WATER THAT IS MILKY OR BLACK: This serious condition indicates the presence of decomposing materials or pollutants. To solve this ptoblem, you'll have to empty your pool and refill it.

OILY FILM This is usually a by-product of decaying leaves, either from the aquatic plants or from nearby trees or shrubs. Lay sheets of newspaper on the water to absorb the oil; this will only take a few minutes. In the future, keep after the problem by pruning your plants regularly and skimming out foliage that falls or blows into the water.

SILT A layer of organic muck inevitably accumulates on the bottom of a pool over time, and it is part of a balanced pond environment. If it seems excessive, scoop out some once each month during the summer.

MAIL-ORDER SUPPLIERS

A local garden center that carries everything needed, and which offers a good selection of plants and supplies is still, unfortunately, a rarity for most water gardeners. Shop by mail for the best selection. Note that many of the following suppliers are small businesses who charge a small fee, usually one to three dollars, for their catalogs. Often, this fee is credited toward your first purchase.

Lilypons Water Gardens
P.O. Box 10
Lilypons, MD 21717

Lilies of the Valley Water Gardens
26585 Rancho San Carlos Road
Carmel, CA 93923

Paradise Water Gardens
14 May Street
Whitman, MA 02382

Perry's Water Gardens
191 Leatherman Gap Road
Franklin, NC 28734

J. Scherer & Sons
104 Waterside Avenue
Northport, NY 11768

Slocum Water Gardens
1101 Cypress Gardens Boulevard
Winter Haven, FL 33880

Stigall Water Gardens
7306 Main Street
Kansas City, MO 64114

TetraPond
201 Tabor Road
Morris Plains, NJ 07950

William Tricker, Inc.
P.O. Box 31267
Independence, OH 44131

Van Ness Water Gardens
2460 North Euclid Avenue
Upland, CA 91786

Waterford Gardens
74 East Allendale Road
Saddle River, NJ 07458

Wicklein's Aquatic Nursery
1820 Cromwell Bridge Road
Baltimore, MD 21234

WATER GARDENING NETWORKS AND RESOURCES

International Water Lily Society
P.O. Box 2309
Columbia, MD 21045
(410)730-8396
Annual membership dues: $21. This includes a subscription to the quarterly journal and invitations to annual and local symposia and tours, and access to reference library, slides, and speakers. The IWLS can alert you to any local societies in your area.

National Pond Society
P.O. Box 449
Acworth, GA 30101
(404) 975-0277
Annual membership dues: $24. This includes a subscription to a magazine, invitations to shows and tours, and access to a reference library.

Water gardening on the Internet

Start with the IWLS's official site: http://h20lily.rain.com
(Best viewed with Netscape software.)
Designed and maintained by IWLS member Jack Honeycutt of Portland, OR. It contains information about joining, an amazing "live videocam view" of his backyard water garden, and an extensive list of other spots on the Internet that will be of interest to water gardeners ("links")— some of them from as far away as Japan and Germany. With a press of a button or a click of the mouse you can jump to any of the listed sites.

If you subscribe to America Online, Prodigy, or Compuserve, check their interest groups under "gardening" or "gardening message boards." Lots of water gardening chatter is going on out there!

Periodicals

The Water Gardener
East-West Specialties
P.O. Box 6004
Norfolk, VA 23508
(804) 461-0665
A full-size, 16-page magazine, produced on a computer and written by a very knowledgeable nurseryman. Reports on latest technology and information on plants, fish, and products; offers expert advice; provides updates on laws and regulations.

Water Gardening
1670 South 900 East
Zionsville, IN 46077
(317) 769-3149
A full-size, 96–114 page magazine, with loads of full-color photographs of plants and pools. This brand-new resource is the result of a collaboration between several Midwestern water-garden experts, and includes articles from around the nation and the world. Monthly columns, plus lots of news, advice, and inspiration. Also includes new-product reviews and ads from which to shop.

Public water garden displays
to visit
Denver Botanic Gardens
909 York Street
Denver, CO 80206
(303) 370-8036

Kenilworth Aquatic Garden
National Capital Parks East
1900 Anacostia Drive S.E.
Washington, DC 20020
(202) 426-6905

Longwood Gardens
Kennett Square, PA 19348
(215) 388-6741

Missouri Botanic Gardens
4344 Shaw Boulevard
St. Louis, MO 63110
(314) 577-5100

Stapeley Water Gardens
Nantwich, Cheshire CW5 7LH
England
0207-623868

Plant Hardiness Zones

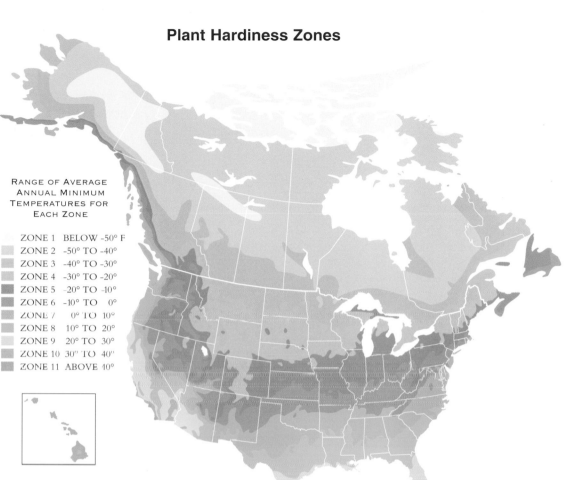

RANGE OF AVERAGE ANNUAL MINIMUM TEMPERATURES FOR EACH ZONE

ZONE 1 BELOW −50° F
ZONE 2 −50° TO −40°
ZONE 3 −40° TO −30°
ZONE 4 −30° TO −20°
ZONE 5 −20° TO −10°
ZONE 6 −10° TO   0°
ZONE 7   0° TO 10°
ZONE 8   10° TO 20°
ZONE 9   20° TO 30°
ZONE 10 30° TO 40°
ZONE 11 ABOVE 40°

FURTHER READING

Heriteau, Jacqueline, and Charles B. Thomas. *Water Gardens.* Boston: Houghton-Mifflin, 1994.

Nash, Helen. *The Pond Doctor.* New York: Sterling Publishing Co., 1994.

Stapeley Water Gardens and Frances Perry. *Waterlilies and Other Aquatic Plants.* New York: Henry Holt and Co., 1989.

Swindells, Philip. *Garden Pools, Waterfalls and Fountains.* London: Ward Lock, 1995.

————. *Small-Garden Pools.* London: Ward Lock, 1992.

Thomas, Charles B. *Water Gardens for Plants and Fish.* Neptune City, N.J.: TFH Publications, 1988.

Tomocik, Joseph V. *The American Garden Guides: Water Gardening.* New York: Pantheon Books, 1996.

Uber, William C. *Water Gardening Basics.* Upland, Calif.: Dragonflyer Press, 1988.

INDEX

Algae, 8, 20, 21, 36, 60, 64, *65*, 68–71, *69*, 85, 92, 94, 96, 99, 118, 119, 121–125

Balance, 63–64, 121

Cannas, *67, 69, 77*, 78, 98, *113*
Cattails, *15*, 77–78, 117

Debris, *37*, 38–40, *41*, 45, 52, 71, 79, 84, 94, 96, 99, 120–121

Electricity, 43, 46, 99, 120–121

Fences, 12, 38, 45, 46, 98
Fertilizer, 8, 9, 36, *69*, 72, 74–76, 82–85, 92, 112, 124
Filters, 53–54, 91, 120, 122, 125
Fish, 11, *18*, 19, 22, 47, 63–64, 96–99, 119, 120
    culture, 9, 12, 17, *18*, 19, *37*, 45, *51*, 53–54, 56, *69*, 70–71, 84–87, 89–90, 92, 94, 121–125
    koi, *18*, 19, *56*, 71, 122
Floaters, 14, 77–78, *104*
    culture, 72, 76, 117–119
Focal points, *25*, 33, *43*
Fountains, *15,* 19, *24–25*, 30, 33, 44, 45, 46, 91, 120, 121, 123, 125
Frogs, 70, 71

Grasses, 70–71, *71*, 78, 98, 115

Hail, 95
Heaters, *89*, 90
Horsetails, *61*, 77, 114

Ice, 86–87, *87, 89*, 90–91, 123
Irises, *15, 16, 17, 59, 65, 67*, 77–79, 92, 115

Leaf spot, 95
Lighting, 89, 121

Liners, 14, 19, 26, 29, 94
    color, 21
    deterioration, *29, 37*, 43, *51*, 54–55, 98–99
    free–form, 20, 49–53, *50–51*, 55
    installation, *48*, 49–53, *50–51*
    liner lingo, 21
    patching, 99
    preformed, 19, *26*, 47, 49, 53
Lotuses, 18, 76–77, 84, 110–112, *112*

Marginals, 36, 46, 60–61, *61*, 77–78, 94, 98
    culture, 70, 72, 75–76, 84, 87–89, 112–117
    on shelves, 20, 33, 75
    in tubs, 14, *15, 17*

Nets, 40

Oxygenating plants, 14, 64, 69–71, 120, 123
    culture, 76, 119
Oxygenation, 45, 53–54, 84–85, *87*, 90, 94, 120, 122–123, 125

Pesticides, 8, 36, 53–54, 56, 125
Pests, *37*, 95–96
    aphids, 94–95
    birds, 21, 43, 96–98
    cats, 17, 99
    China Mark moth, 95
    crown rot, 95
    mosquitoes, 17, 71, 121–122
    muskrats, 21, 43, 82, 98
    raccoons, 21, 43, 98
    on shelves, 21
    turtles, 98
pH conditions, 22, 29, *30*, 38, 40, *51*, 53–54, 56, 71, *75*, 76, 85, 99, 122–123, 125
Plants, *18*, 30, 33, *41*, 43, 45, 47, 82, 85
    color choices, 77–78

Plants (*continued*)
    culture, 14–17, *29*, 53–54, 56, 72–77, 84
    pot selection, 14–17, 72–73, 76, 82, 111
    selection, 59–60, *61–63*, 76–79, 101–119
Pools, 8, 12–19
    above–ground, *28*, 29
    capacity calculation, 47, 120
    concrete, 22, *23*
    container, 8, *12*, 12–19, *13–17*
    depth, 11, *18*, 19, 44, 46
    dimensions, 46–48
    draining, 92–94, 120
    edging, 20, *35*, 36–37, *37, 51*, 53, *54–55*, 56, 78–79, 99
    formal, *11*, 29, *30–31*
    free–form, 46–47, 52, 56
    garden, *11*, 33, *37*
    informal, *11*, 33
    in–ground, *29–30*
    installation, 48–52, *50–51*
    landscaping, 14, 33, *71*, 78–79, *81*
    leveling, *37*, 41, *50*, 52, 56
    liners, 14, 19, 20, 21, 26, 29
    locating, 12, 35, 36, 40–46, *43, 50*
    metal, 18–19
    preformed, 19, 47, 49
    shape, *11*, 20, 30, 33, 46, *50*
    shelves, 20–21, 33, 70, 75, 96, 120
    size, *11*, 12, 19, 38
    surface area calculation, 47
    surface coverage, 60, *65*, 68–71, 96,
    wooden, 14–17, 56, 72
Primroses, *67*, 79
Pumps, *12*, 19, 20, 24, *25*, 26, 46, 47, 90, 94, 120–121, 125

Rain, 22, 29, 35

Safety, 43–44, 46, 120
Scavengers, 71, 94, 99, 125

Shade, 18, *37*, 38, *43*, 68, 70
Silt, 36, 126
Soils, 19, 22, 30, 43, 52, 79, 94
    for potted plants, 72–73, *74*, 76
Statuary, 29, *30, 33*, 43
Sun
    deterioration from, 19, 20, *29*, 30,*37, 51*, 54–55, 99
    plant requirements, 18, 30, *35*, 36–38, *39, 50*, 68–69, *69*, 77, 84, 102, 111
    protection from, 12, 29, 92

Trees and shrubs, *26*, 37–40, *41*, 95

Water
    pool requirements, 8, 46, 47, 53–54, 84–85, 94
    quality, 60, 124–126
    runoff into pool, *15*, 29, 30, 36–37, *37*, 38, 41, 49, 124
Waterfalls, *26–27*, 33, 44, 45, 46, 91, 120, 121, 123, 125
Waterlilies, 8, *11*, 33, *35, 59*, 60, 77–78, 81, 94, 98, *101*
    culture, 9, 16, 17, 20, 24, *26*, 30, 36, 38, *39*, 45–46, 59, *61, 65*, 68–71, *69*, 72–75, 84–85, 87–89, 91–92, *93*, 95, 102–110, 121
    hybridizing, 103
Water temperature, 12, 18, 19, 20, 29, 38, 45, 54, 69, 71, 74–76, *82*, 85, *87, 89*, 89–92, 94, 111, 120, 123, 124
Wind and air, 12, 44–46, 111, 123
Winter, 19, *81, 82–87*, 94–95
    plant preparation, 85–91, 105, 111, 119
    pool deterioration, 20, 22, *23*, 53
    pool preparation, 22, 29, 90–91, 120, 123